THE
SCARBOROUGH PLAN

Maximizing the Power of Your 401(k)

J. Michael Scarborough

CORINTHIAN
BOOKS

Mt. Pleasant, S.C.

Publishers Cataloging-in-Publication Data
(Provided by Quality Books)

Scarborough, J. Michael.
    The Scarborough plan : maximizing the power of your 401(k) / J. Michael Scarborough. — 1st ed.
        p. cm.
    LCCN: 00-101448
    ISBN: 1-929175-18-3

    1. Finance, Personal. 2. 401(k) plans.
3. Retirement—United States—Planning.
4. Investments.   I. Title.

HG179.S37 2000   332.024'01
                                  QBI00-500109

Corinthian Books
An imprint of
The Côté Literary Group
P. O. Box 1898
Mt. Pleasant, S.C. 29465-1898
(843) 881-6080
http://www.corinthianbooks.com

To my children, Katie and Matthew,
who have inspired me to succeed.

ACKNOWLEDGMENTS

As I have traveled the country conducting seminars and lectures on 401(k) and retirement planning, I have learned that it is always good to come home to the friends and the family that you truly care about. It is those friends that you can depend on most to help you accomplish your goals. I believe I have the greatest friends in the world!

The creation of this book would not have been possible without the assistance, advice, and guidance of my good friends and colleagues at The Scarborough Group. I have many people to thank for their help with this book.

My Retirement Advisors have proved themselves to be the best in the business with the caring, attentive way in which they advise clients. Along with my Research Department, they provided advice and input vital to the publication of this book. My Administration Team is the backbone of The Scarborough Group, and without their diligence, we would not be where we are today.

My Marketing Department helps 401(k) participants understand our savings plan management service. My Information Technology Department is always creating new ways to take 401(k) advice and asset management into the future. And my Management Team keeps the company moving forward with their vision.

Finally, I owe great thanks to Marianne Leedy, my Vice President of Education and Development, who is truly my closest advisor, dear friend, and voice of reason. Her dedication and efforts in the development of this book will forever be appreciated.

CONTENTS

FOREWORD

There was a time when people would say buying a house was the biggest investment most of us ever made. Today, managing your retirement plan through your 401(k) is the most important investment any of us have. For some Americans, their 401(k) contributory savings plan is the only retirement savings they have known. For others, it has replaced other benefit programs which we once had but never had to manage. For all of us, managing our savings and understanding and using our plan is essential to retirement.

Investing for retirement involves more than adding pennies to the cookie jar each week. It means managing your money by understanding how much you can set aside for investments, how much you need to invest, and what investments are available to you. Moreover, 401(k) plans are a start, but are not always the finish. It is important to understand what it can and can't do and how you should use it. Sometimes it is also useful to know how your plan differs from other tax-deferred retirement plans or whether your plan has all the options allowed by the laws and regulations.

The key steps in thinking about retirement are to understand your needs and how to begin investing, and most of all, understand something about asset allocation and how to invest. Once you've got that start, you need to know what you can and can't do through your 401(k) and how to find other plans that will complement your 401(k). Finally, once you get there, you need to know what to do with your money when you do retire. Mike Scarborough and The Scarborough Group have a lot of experience working with 401(k) plans and similar retirement plans. They know investing, know 401(k) plans, and how plans work and what can be done with them.

Since most of us haven't retired yet—and probably will only retire once—we may not be experts in how to do it successfully. So, some of us may need some help along the way. This is a good place to start.

—David M. Blitzer
Managing Director, Standard & Poor's

PREFACE

At one of my retirement seminars recently, a man in the sixth row timidly stood up, nervously looked around, and asked, "Mr. Scarborough, my name is Stan. What exactly *is* retirement?"

The woman in the first row—his company's Human Resources Director—rolled her eyes and shook her head in disbelief. The man sitting next to Stan stared up at him with a "what-an-idiot" frown on his face. Low-level snickering flowed across the room like "the wave" at a ball game.

After the room quieted down, and after Stan crawled back out from under his chair where he had taken refuge from the scorn of his fellow employees, I looked at him and said, "Stan, my man, you are the true hero of this seminar. You had the guts to ask the question that almost no one here knows the answer to yet. I am *so* glad you asked—and they should be, too." Stan grinned.

We give retirement planning seminars all the time, and it never ceases to amaze me how few people know what they mean when they start talking retirement. Try to pin them down, and they start talking ages—fifty-five, sixty-five, whenever. Or they start counting years—five years from now, twenty years from now, or "as soon as I can," that sort of thing. Even then, they're talking in generalities. They're not talking about *their* retirement, they're talking about "well, you know, just retirement."

So here's something you need to understand right off the bat. Retirement is not an age. Retirement is not an event. Retirement is a phase you go through after you quit working where you've been working full-time for however many years. And with any luck, it's a phase you'll spend twenty or thirty or more years enjoying. Enjoying, that is, if you figure out how to pay for it before you get there. That's what this book is all about: how to maximize the advantages of your company-sponsored 401(k) program so that you can retire and live the rest of your life enjoying a high standard of living, ***no matter how long you live.***

Nobody buys a book like this for the joy of learning abstract or complex economic or financial theories. I assume you are here to learn how to achieve financial security so that you can retire when you want to and maintain a comfortable standard of living for the rest of your life. For that reason, there is little economic or financial theory in this book.

This book starts with basic retirement planning at the "Stan" level, then gives you the information and tools you need to maximize the power of your 401(k) retirement plan. In a clear, simple, and step-by-step manner, I will cover all the major aspects of financial planning for your retirement, how to evaluate and optimize the financial power of your 401(k), and how to best work with a financial planner to achieve your goals. Finally, I'll show you how to make the most effective use of your assets once you do retire.

When working with my clients, I have no place for the "cookie-cutter approach" to retirement planning. You won't get any of that in this book, either. Everything I'll give you will enable you to do what's best for *you* and *your* loved ones — not for some faceless group of people that happen to be your age or follow your profession.

In these pages you'll find some ideas and recommendations that seem to fly in the face of "conventional wisdom" about retirement planning. Some do — with good reason: a fair amount of retirement planning information passed off as "conventional wisdom" is either obsolete (much of it dragged along, useful or not, from two and three generations ago) or was fundamentally flawed in the first place. If so, I'll tell you so, and tell you why the information here is better.

The Scarborough Plan consists of five key components, all of which will be carefully explained and illustrated.

The Scarborough Plan

1. Define in detail your retirement lifestyle.
2. Calculate exactly how much you'll need in your retirement account.
3. Determine how long it will be before you must tap into your retirement assets.
4. Start saving the required amounts now.
5. As you progress through the stages of your retirement, draw upon your assets according to a prioritized plan.

Everything you'll find here is practical knowledge you can immediately put into use. All of it comes directly from my own training as a financial and investment counselor, from the insights I've gained helping my clients grow their retirement portfolios, and from the experience of the senior staff, securities specialists, and investment planners at The Scarborough Group, Inc.

I hope you find it useful.

                                    J. Michael Scarborough

SECTION I
THE BASICS OF
RETIREMENT PLANNING

WHAT YOU NEED FOR A RICH RETIREMENT

Retirement begins when you cease relying on your company or business or organization to figure out for you how you'll spend your days. Sometimes you have the pleasure of deciding when that happens. Other times higher powers determine the fate of your future. Regardless of how it happens, when you retire, you're no longer working at the job that you've loved or hated or merely tolerated for longer than you can remember.

What happens next depends upon what you want to do or what you must do, based largely on how well you've planned up to that point. Three basic stages of retirement face you, and you may end up passing through any or all three stages before you graduate from retirement to, well, death.

Stage I

Stage One is for those of you who still work—maybe part-time, maybe full-time—after you've started retiring. Lots of folks start second careers, turn their hobbies into income-producing businesses, or simply enjoy the social interactions they get working at a job which is totally different from their previous one. The point is that many people still work in some capacity during their early retirement. The work provides some income, so they have less need to dip into whatever assets they've accumulated during their *real* working life. And that's the great benefit of this retirement stage if you've planned it right: not only do you forego withdrawals from your retirement assets, but you also allow those assets to continue growing, promising you an even wealthier retirement a few more years down the road.

Face it, though. Some of you end up in this stage (or may already be here) as a result of poor planning along the way. The good news is, there's still time. Not much, mind you, but always some. Applying sound investment principles—following a good plan—can shorten the amount of time you must spend in this still-working-but-retired stage of your life. More than anyone else, you need to get your plan formulated and begin executing it. *NOW.*

Stage II

Which brings us to the second stage. Now you've finished working, *really* finished working. No more hawking your jewelry at craft shows, no more consulting, no more "would you like fries with that?" Because of judicious spending and, with any luck, accumulating some assets you don't need anymore—that five-bedroom house, for example—you don't need to tap those still-growing retirement resources. Instead, you can use up some of those cash reserves that aren't earning much income anyway, sell the house and live off some of the proceeds (investing the rest), auction off that Andy Warhol painting you never liked anyhow. You get the picture. Almost everybody passes through this stage. For lots of reasons we'll get into later, you want to delay as much as possible your need to begin withdrawing from your accumulated retirement assets.

Stage III

Eventually you reach the third stage. You may have liquidated all the assets you want to liquidate. You may have drawn down your cash reserves to a level below which you're not comfortable. Or you may have reached the second legal age in your life, the one where you **must** start taking withdrawals from one or all of your retirement accounts. At this point, you will be fully reliant on the income created by the assets you've accumulated in all the prior years. Your retirement planning doesn't end at this point. You still must be able to implement a strategy of withdrawal that maximizes your cash flow, minimizes your taxes, and maintains—so far as possible—the principal amounts in your retirement accounts.

It's this third stage—and when you plan to reach it—that's most critical in all the planning we'll talk about. You need to know when you'll first need your retirement monies, because the amount of time between now and then determines everything from how much you need to set aside on a regular basis to how you invest what you do set aside. Starting now is critically important. A dollar you invest today is worth more than a dollar you invest tomorrow. The sooner you start investing, the longer you will have till you reach stage three—more time for you to contribute, and more time for it to grow.

No Goals, No Glory

A couple came into the office the other day. He was forty-five, she was forty-two. They have three kids, all teenagers.

"Geoff and I want to retire when we're fifty-five," said Sharon. "Quit completely and live off our retirement money." She'd already heard my definition of retirement.

"Great," I said. "And then what?"

"What do you mean?" Geoff asked.

"And then what will you do?" I asked again. "Where will you live? What will you do with your time? What about the kids? What *exactly* are your plans?"

It was an awkward silence. A very typical awkward silence.

Here's a basic principle: if you don't know where you're

headed, you're never going to get anywhere. This rule applies to everything from education to driving to sailing to, well, to retirement planning. And I don't mean some fuzzy notion of where you think you might like to end up; I mean planning, right down to the last detail. Just as you shouldn't plan to go to college to get a degree—any degree—you shouldn't have a retirement plan that goes something like this: "We'd like to travel, maybe play some golf, see the grandkids." Imagine your kids saying, "I'd like to go to college, maybe take some courses, get a degree." You'd sit them down and have a long, serious talk.

You must know what you want in order to achieve it. Make a list of very specific, detailed retirement goals. Include all the things that you might not necessarily want, but that you might need somewhere along the way.

Take some time to sit down and have a long, serious talk with the person who will share your retirement years. Remember: you must know what you want in order to achieve it.

Make a list of very specific, detailed retirement goals. Include things that you might not necessarily want, but that you might need (such as assisted living facilities) somewhere along the way. Be as complete and as specific as you can.

What about a new house? You said earlier that you no longer need all this room for just the two of you and your fourteen-year-old Labrador retriever. How big will the new house be? How much should you spend for it? Where will it be? What are the property taxes like there? Will the water bill where you're going be the same as the one where you live now? Higher? Lower? All these questions need answers.

Or maybe several homes. That condo on the golf course looks nice. And how about that cabin in the mountains for those autumn colors? How much will those cost? What will maintenance expenses be when you're not there? Can you recover some of those expenses by renting them when you're not around?

When you are listing the place(s) you'll live, don't forget those other short-term "residences" you've had your eyes on. The boat you want to buy—whether it's a sixteen-foot fishing boat or a sixty-five-foot yacht—will have to be included in your budget, as will the motor home, the camping trailer, or the LearJet. All these things cost money. Write them down.

It seems as though everyone who talks about retirement talks about travel. When you're planning your retirement years, be specific in the type of travel you'd like to do. That way, you'll either be sure of affording it or aware (before the disappointment) that it's impossible with your budget. Where exactly do you want to travel? To visit the grandkids? The Grand Canyon? The Grand Canal in Venice? The three-week cooking school in the South of France? And when you go, where will you stay? In a campground? In a cheap motel? In a castle? Where and how you travel makes a big difference in your retirement planning. Be specific.

Education costs money, too. Will your kids be finished with college? Will you be finished paying for it? Maybe you'd like to go back to school yourself, now that your college finally offers that Ph.D. in fly-fishing techniques. Or perhaps you've promised the grandkids you'll fund their medical education at Harvard (there goes the yacht!). Maybe education belongs on your list, maybe not.

Just in case you haven't checked lately, weddings and honeymoons can set you back big bucks. Will your kids be grown and married off before you retire, or not? If not, be sure to include the expense of her wedding or his honeymoon in your planning. Either that or start instilling in them now the financial virtues of elopement and the intimacy of camping.

While you're at it, this is the time to work those less pleasant contingencies into your retirement planning goals. Think about any chronic medical conditions you have and what they'll cost over the twenty or thirty years of your retirement. Consider the health of your parents—even if you're healthy now, you're probably susceptible to some of the same diseases and conditions that affect them. They are you, twenty or twenty-five years down the road.

Many people live independently right up till the day they die. Others don't. Might you or your spouse require some sort of sheltered retirement living? Could a nursing home be in your future? You can never know for sure what your medical or daily living requirements will be years from now, but you can anticipate those possibilities and plan for them.

These are but a few of the things that you should consider listing among your retirement plans and goals. A more complete—but still not exhaustive—list of items you might include the following.

Things to Consider in Your Retirement Planning

♦ Where will you live? In your existing home? In a smaller home? In several homes?

♦ What will you drive? How often will you replace your car? Will you buy new or used?

♦ What "luxury" items will you buy? A boat? A yacht? A recreational vehicle? A chalet in Switzerland?

♦ What medical expenses might you encounter? Chronic medications? Home health care? Nursing home care? Hospitalization?

♦ Will you provide financial assistance to your parents, children, or grandchildren?

♦ What happens to your retirement picture if your

spouse dies? What if you divorce? If you're single, what if you marry?

♦ Will you travel after you retire? In what style? How often? To where? For how long?

♦ Will you want to contribute to charities? Establish your own foundation?

♦ Will you have other debts that must be taken into account?

♦ Do you expect to spend more time learning about finances and managing your own money – or will you need to find a good advisor?

The things which are most important in establishing your goals are completeness and detail. In your planning, you need to be able to make a place for every one of your goals. To do that, you need to know what they are. To achieve the goals, you must know exactly what the goals require. Otherwise, you might find yourself hunting for bear with nothing but a slingshot. The goal is specific enough — but not the planning and preparation.

The bottom line: if you want to enjoy a good retirement, know exactly what you intend to do while you're living it. Figure it out. Write it down. And don't leave anything out.

You Didn't Pick Your Birthday, Either

If you've ever read a book or attended a seminar about retirement planning, you know that people can spend a lot of time predicting how long you'll live and, based on that and your goals, how much you'll need to set aside to do what you want before you die. They'll pull out the life expectancy tables and tell you that if you're a fifty-seven-year-old white woman today that you'll probably live until you're about seventy-nine, but that if you're already seventy, you could live until you're eighty-five.

Or if they're really high-tech, they'll plug in your age, your education level, your income, the age at which your grandparents died, whether you smoke, and how much you weigh into their computer program and tell you exactly how long you'll live.

Baloney. You can look at all the life expectancy tables in the world or employ any piece of software in existence; none of them will tell you exactly when you'll die.

So here's what I recommend: forget about all this how-old-you-are nonsense. As I said earlier, just figure out when you'll need the cash flow. As I'll explain later, the best approach to retirement planning is this: plan on the assumption that you will live forever. At least then you won't run out of cash before you run out of days.

The best approach to retirement planning is this: plan on the assumption that you will live forever. At least then you won't run out of cash before you run out of days.

Recognizing that not everyone has the resources to put away enough principal to live forever off its proceeds, I generally recommend that you at least overestimate your life expectancy. Here's a good rule of thumb: figure out the oldest age at which one of your close relatives—parent, grandparent, or sibling—died. Now add ten years to that. Use this estimated life expectancy to determine how long you'd have to rely on your retirement resources if you were to use up every dime.

Still, if you start early enough and save wisely, many of you *will* be able to reach the goal of having sufficient principal invested to live comfortably forever.

Allocation, Allocation, Allocation

One of my retirement advisers came to me with this situation:

"Mike," she said, "Mr. Williams wants us to help him manage his 401(k). He says he knows *all* about asset allocation."

I immediately thought, *Here we go.*

She continued, "He said, 'Since I'm forty-five now, I need to be 60% in stock, 30% in bonds, and 10% in cash.'"

I could tell from the look on her face that she disagreed with him, but that Mr. Williams apparently held his opinions with some conviction.

"So what do I tell him?" she asked.

You guessed it. It doesn't matter how old you are. What matters is this: how long will it be before you need to start taking withdrawals from your retirement savings? The generational approach to asset allocation — how you split your investment dollars among the different types of investments based solely upon your age — makes no sense whatsoever. Are you going to need your retirement savings at the same time as everyone else your age? Probably not. Are you going to be comfortable—at any age—with the same asset mix as somebody else you know? Maybe, maybe not.

Your best bet is to throw out the whole notion of allocating your investment dollars according to your age, along with the life expectancy tables. There's no place for this kind of cookie-cutter approach to retirement planning.

I have found that it's best to have three different types of retirement portfolios, based on how far you are from needing the proceeds (stage three of your retirement).

♦ Portfolio A: If you are more than 12 years away from needing the cash flow.

♦ Portfolio B: If you are between 5 and 12 years of needing the cash flow.

♦ Portfolio C: If you are within 5 years of needing the cash flow.

Notice again that these divisions have nothing to do with how old you are or how old you're going to be or when you die.

Figure out when stage three of your retirement will begin. That's the stage where you no longer earn an income and you must rely on whatever you've put aside to live according to the plans you made. From that time you can count backwards in years to determine how to allocate your investment dollars. It's as simple as that.

Portfolio A: Aggressive Growth

If you won't be drawing on your retirement assets for twelve years or more, you should have a retirement portfolio with an aggressive allocation of assets. The investments should be heavily tilted toward growth stocks, including stocks of smaller companies. All the historical data support a diversified portfolio substantially, if not exclusively, invested in growth stocks.

Portfolio B: Moderately Aggressive

In the interval between twelve and five years before you need retirement income, your portfolio should reflect moderately aggressive allocations. It should certainly include a substantial number of growth stocks (or growth stock funds), as well as some of the income-producing elements that will make up your conservative portfolio at the end of this period. Throughout this interval, the allocation of assets should be changed gradually from a more aggressive mix (emphasizing growth stocks) to a more conservative mix (emphasizing value stocks, dividend-paying stocks, and bonds) as you get closer to your actual retirement phase.

Portfolio C: Fairly conservative

When you are within five years of needing income from your retirement savings, your portfolio of assets should become fairly conservative in their allocation. At this stage, and throughout your retirement, you want to be assured of an income stream with a minimal risk of losing the value of your principal. For this reason, your portfolio should include such assets as dividend-paying stocks (or funds), stocks or funds with a consistent history of paying dividends, high-grade corporate bonds (or funds), and U.S. Treasury instruments.

Exactly how the assets of your portfolio should best be allocated at any time depends upon a number of factors. We'll explore asset allocation in detail in Chapter 3. For now, it's enough to know that as you get closer to needing your retirement income, you will need to take steps to protect your retirement principal from the vagaries and fluctuations of the stock markets. You will do this—probably with the help of an advisor—by focusing less on volatile assets like stocks and more on stable assets like bonds.

Don't Believe Everything You Hear

One of the questions I hear most frequently is this: "How much money will I need when I retire?"

My answer: "More than you've been led to believe." Talk to just about any investment advisor or open any retirement planning book and you'll be told that you'll need anywhere from 60% to 80% of your pre-retirement income after you retire. They justify this range because of your presumed lower cost of living now that you're commuting less, saving that $50 a month on dry cleaning, buying fewer lunches, and so on.

To all this I say **rubbish.**

Just a while back you finished writing that list of goals to work towards during your retirement. Achieving those goals will cost money. Chances are, for every expense you lose when you retire, you'll gain another one. You'll likely spend more money on travel than you did before, at least enough to match those commuting savings. And when you're traveling, you'll spend all that saved lunch money on meals around the world. All right, maybe you *will* save a few dollars on dry cleaning, but 20% of your income? Not likely.

What about those expenses that you don't have now but that will arise later? Older people—and you'll almost certainly be older when you retire—spend more on health care and medicines than any other age group. Virtually any long-term supervised living accommodations or nursing home care costs more than whatever you're spending now on housing. Think things through. For every job-related expense you won't have after you retire you can probably identify a matching expense you'll face at some point during your retirement years.

Here's an easy rule of thumb about your post-retirement cash flow requirements: plan on 100% of your pre-retirement cash flow. Not only is it better to have too much rather than too little, but also you must plan for unforeseen contingencies. You also have to deal with the inevitable erosion of the value of your money by inflation. And don't forget the "savings" part of your budget. It's far better to pay cash for that new car than to take a hit on your monthly cash flow. For all the reasons I've mentioned, then, your best bet is to plan on needing just as much money after you retire as you do now.

Here's an easy rule of thumb about your post-retirement cash flow requirements: plan on 100% of your pre-retirement cash flow. Not only is it better to have too much rather than too little, but also you must plan for unforeseen contingencies.

You need a cash flow figure to figure out how much principal you'll need to have invested for your retirement. To arrive at that figure, take your current monthly (or yearly) income and grow it by 3% (for inflation) compounded annually for every year between now and the time you will need the cash flow. Here's a table that does that for you for a selected number of years. Just multiply the value in the table by the number of thousands you think you'll need for a given period.

Remember that this represents income, not savings. In the next section, you'll learn how much you'll

How long until you need the money	How much you'll need per $1000 in today's dollars
1 year	$1,030
3 years	$1,093
5 years	$1,159
10 years	$1,344
15 years	$1,558
20 years	$1,806

have to have set aside in order to supply this sort of income. The point here is that you'll need the same number of dollars after you retire as you need now—adjusted for inflation. If anyone suggests otherwise, ask him how you'll reach all those retirement goals you've established by spending less money than you live on today. Go ahead, ask him.

Plan to Live Forever

"All right," you're thinking, "you've told me how much income I'll need from my investments, but you haven't told me how long I'll need it."

Unless you skipped the beginning of this chapter, you already know what I think about life expectancy forecasts. Nevertheless, you're bound to find any number of advisors who tell you that you need to save enough to last you until you're—well, however old the tables say you'll be. In other words, they'll advise you to have just enough money to last you till the day you die. Maybe the day after. In other words, die broke.

Planning to die broke is unwise for at least two reasons. First, it ignores all those whom you care about who will outlive you. Unless your spouse happens to die the same time you do—and that happens only in those rare circumstances where people suffer accidental deaths or planned mutual deaths, neither of which most people can count on—you'll have to leave enough for him or her to live on till he or she finally exits. I'd also venture to guess that most of you would like to leave a little financial legacy for your children or your grandchildren or—who knows?— your pet. Maybe you've always wanted to have a building at your alma mater named after you. Perhaps you have a favorite charity that you'd like to receive a portion of your estate. So you probably don't want to plan on exhausting all your retirement resources before you die.

Second, planning to die broke requires you to die at just the right time. This, of course, is fraught with problems. You either have to know exactly when that's going to be—neither an easy nor a pleasant task—or you have to see to it that you actually *do* die when the planned-for day arrives. While the second choice is achievable, I can't imagine many people opting for it.

Your only reasonable alternative, then, is to plan as though you're going to live forever. Plan your retirement as though you will never die. Never.

The way to make your income last forever—even if you don't happen to live forever—is to plan to live solely off the income generated by your investments. Plan to have enough invested so that you never have to dip into the principal amount itself. In fact, plan for your principal to generate enough income to meet your cash flow requirements and to keep pace with inflation, both without diminishing the principal itself. This approach assures that you will have a perpetual income, one that grows in step with inflation, and that money will be left over for your heirs when you finally die. What more could you ask for?

Oh, yes. An amount. To determine how much you'll need to have set aside, you'll need two things. First, you need to know how much income you need on a regular basis. You should have determined that amount from the earlier exercise in growing your current income requirements for inflation. Second, you need to make some assumptions about the rate your investments will earn and the rate of inflation during your retirement years. For our purposes, we'll accept some historically reasonable figures for earnings and inflation rates. Over a long investment horizon—say five years or so—your investments should be able to grow at an average annual rate of 8.5%. Historically, inflation in the United States averages about 3% per year. Simple math says that your investments will give you 5.5% in income after you reinvest the 3% needed to keep up with inflation.

Now that you know the assumptions, here are the results. On page 18 you'll find out how much money you will have to have invested by the time you retire in order to realize the perpetual income desired. Now all that remains is to figure out how to get that much money put away in the years you have remaining before you need it.

No doubt you're also curious how much you'll have to set aside on a monthly or yearly basis in order to achieve the principal targets above. For that calculation—it's a bit more complicated—let's assume the same ability to earn 8.5% annually on your investment over the period from now until you need to start withdrawing funds. Naturally, investing monthly beats investing yearly, because all those monthly additions are growing throughout the rest of the year. On the next page are a few examples of what you need to invest to reach your target.

As I said earlier, this is the ideal approach—one which may not prove practical for everybody. Once you work through the ideal scenario, if the amounts you arrive at seem impossible for you, don't worry. You can also arrive at a target savings amount by using the life expectancy rule of thumb I gave you before: your oldest relative plus ten years.

Here's one simple, conservative way to be sure you

Regular income you need	Principal required to provide it
$ 1,000	$ 18,182
$ 5,000	$ 90,909
$ 10,000	$ 181,818
$ 20,000	$ 363,636
$ 50,000	$ 909,091
$100,000	$1,818,182

have the retirement assets you need in the non-ideal world. To compensate for the *fact* of inflation, assume your retirement account will earn nothing from the day you retire till the day you die (I told you this was a conservative approach!). Take your monthly expenses and multiply them by the number of months you've figured you'll live in your third phase of retirement. Increase that amount by 3% (compounded) for every year between now and the time you retire. Then use that figure to arrive at your required "principal" amount and use the tables to determine what you must invest regularly to reach it.

Need an example? Say you spend $4,000 a month, you'll live 21 years after retirement, and you want to retire twenty years from now. You'll need $4,000 times 21 years times 12 months/year = $1,008,000, before adjusting for inflation. Figure in the 3% annually compounded inflation and you get $1,008,000 times 1.8 (trust me on this one), which means you need $1,820,000 or so in principal. According to the "20 years" table above, you need to put away about $2,900 each month between now and then, assuming you're starting from ground zero.

Finally, whenever you're determining the necessary monthly (or annual) investment you must make, don't forget your employer's match (if you have one). The amounts in the tables can be reduced by whatever dollar amount your employer funnels into your 401(k) or other investment account.

Two things should be immediately obvious from this abundance of tables. First, investing a regular amount at

To reach this principal in 5 years	Invest monthly	Invest yearly
$ 10,000	$ 134	$ 1,688
$ 20,000	$ 269	$ 3,375
$ 50,000	$ 672	$ 8,438
$ 100,000	$ 1,343	$ 16,877
$ 500,000	$ 6,717	$ 84,383
$1,000,000	$13,433	$168,766
$2,000,000	$26,866	$337,532

To reach this principal in 10 years	Invest monthly	Invest yearly
$ 10,000	$ 53	$ 674
$ 20,000	$ 106	$ 1,348
$ 50,000	$ 266	$ 3,370
$ 100,000	$ 532	$ 6,741
$ 500,000	$ 2,658	$ 33,704
$1,000,000	$ 5,315	$ 67,408
$2,000,000	$10,630	$134,815

To reach this principal in 15 years	Invest monthly	Invest yearly
$ 10,000	$ 28	$ 354
$ 20,000	$ 55	$ 708
$ 50,000	$ 138	$ 1,771
$ 100,000	$ 276	$ 3,542
$ 500,000	$ 1,382	$ 17,710
$1,000,000	$ 2,764	$ 35,420
$2,000,000	$ 5,528	$ 70,841

To reach this principal in 20 years	Invest monthly	Invest yearly
$ 10,000	$ 16	$ 207
$ 20,000	$ 32	$ 413
$ 50,000	$ 80	$ 1,034
$ 100,000	$ 159	$ 2,067
$ 500,000	$ 797	$ 10,335

| $1,000,000 | $1,595 | $20,671 |
| $2,000,000 | $3,190 | $41,342 |

To reach this principal in **30 years**	Invest **monthly**	Invest **yearly**
$ 10,000	$ 6	$ 81
$ 20,000	$ 12	$ 161
$ 50,000	$ 30	$ 403
$ 100,000	$ 61	$ 805
$ 500,000	$ 303	$ 4,025
$1,000,000	$ 606	$ 8,051
$2,000,000	$1,212	$16,101

the end of each month costs you less than investing regularly at the end of each year. Second, the earlier you start, the less you have to invest on a regular basis to reach your target amount. In other words, save early and save often.

The Well-Worn Path to Failure

Now and then I'll meet a new client whose retirement planning simply has not worked. By and large, the reasons for such failures fall into one of two categories: poor planning or poor execution. They occur in roughly equal proportions.

Poor planning includes both making bad plans and making no plans. Bad planning can come about from following bad advice or simply having no idea where you're headed or how to get there. Bad planning, as we already mentioned, can come from having nebulous goals in mind, rather than definite targets at which you take aim with every investment decision. After you understand The Scarborough Plan, your days of bad planning should be over. You will have definite retirement financial objectives—written down—along with a clear strategy for attaining those objectives.

Making no plans—well, we have already discussed that

enough to cure you of roaming in the general direction of retirement. Even a bad plan beats no plan at all. Make a plan. Write it down. The sooner, the better.

The best retirement planning in the world will fail if you don't follow the plan. I've met people who have paid hundreds of dollars to financial planners or retirement counselors or whatever for the best plans money can buy. Then they do nothing with them. They nod their heads, take their personalized plans home, and lose them in some stack of magazines. I know this sounds crazy, but believe me, you'll find people who just don't follow through—at all.

Nearly as bad as no execution is poor execution. You go through this book, for example, and say to yourself, *What a great plan!*, you get started down the right road to retirement, and then you get sidetracked somewhere along the way. Maybe you don't fully understand the concepts underlying good retirement planning (this book will fix that). Maybe your investments perform badly for one quarter and you lose confidence and move them around without giving it the same careful consideration you gave the original plan. Maybe you simply don't pay attention to what's going on, pursuing the plan with total disregard to what's happening in the financial markets and in the economy. Or maybe you just get weary. Sticking with your plan isn't easy when you're being bombarded with promises of "100% returns in 6 months—guaranteed." If it gives you any comfort, you're not alone. More people fall short of their goals because of poor execution than because of poor planning.

By the time you lay this book down, you'll know everything you need to know about using your 401(k) plan to carry you to a financially secure retirement. But it will be up to you to put that knowledge to work and keep it working for you. Chances are, you'll decide that the execution of your plan takes more time and energy than you have to spend on it. That's okay; at the end of the book, we'll discuss the sort of help that's available to overcome the problem of poor execution.

Getting There from Here

We've spent a lot of time in this chapter discussing the process of planning for a rich retirement and the pitfalls you're likely to encounter along the way. We haven't spent much time considering specifically the question of how you get there from where you are now. So let's finish with three steps you need to follow in order to reach that rich retirement you seek.

First, make good, realistic plans. As far as your 401(k) is concerned, utilize the steps of the Scarborough Plan. It will bring you the best possible growth for your own personal risk tolerance. This book will play a key role, then, in your financial planning for retirement. Read it carefully, understand it thoroughly, and use it to prepare your own retirement plan.

I'd be nuts, though, if I suggested there was nothing to retirement but 401(k) accounts. There's also insurance, IRAs, bank accounts, annuities, Social Security (you hope), inheritances, real estate, and a whole lot else that needs to be figured into your plan. This book doesn't have the space to consider every element of your retirement in great detail. You'll want to consult a retirement counselor, investment advisor, or financial planner to help you craft the other components of your retirement portfolio.

Second, follow your plans carefully. We already discussed the fact that your plan will prove to be only as good as its execution. Follow through on every detail of the plan you formulate. Stick with the regular investment amounts you deemed appropriate to provide you the retirement cash flow you think you'll need. Pay attention to the allocation of assets within your retirement portfolio. If you don't have time to execute your plan carefully, find somebody else to do it. Remember this: it's usually the implementation that fails, not the plan.

Third, reassess your plan periodically. This doesn't mean checking your 401(k) every day and moving money from one asset to another. This could cost you a bundle in brokerage fees (if there are redemption or transaction fees, for example) over the long haul and would likely reduce your returns. It does mean taking a look at the returns of the various assets that make up your portfolio on a regular basis and evaluating whether any balancing needs to take place. Even then, monitoring doesn't necessarily mean modifying. It simply means that you evaluate the returns of the various assets that make up your portfolio to determine whether they're still the best performers within their asset classes—in other words, do you still own the best stocks, bonds, and mutual funds for your particular needs?

How often is "periodically"? Well, it depends. If you're close to retirement, you'll want to monitor your assets more often than you will if you're decades from retiring. Here are some general guidelines, then, about the frequency with which you might be not only assessing, but also reallocating your retirement portfolio.

- Within 5 years of retirement: quarterly. During this period, you will be making finer adjustments to your portfolio to ensure its ability to provide you with the regular cash flow in amounts you find appropriate to your situation.
- Between 5 and 12 years from retirement: quarterly to semiannually. Rather than being concerned about cash flow, you'll want to be sure that each of your asset classes is doing what it needs to do for you: provide the best return for its level of risk.
- More than 12 years from retirement: semiannually to annually. As you will see later, during this period your portfolio will consist mostly—if not exclusively—of growth stocks. Though there may be rare occasions to change the allocation, the real reason for monitoring is to be sure that you have the best growth stocks around.

Building your retirement portfolio may be the most

important project you ever undertake. By now, you should be well on your way to determining exactly the sort of retirement you want. And the style of retirement you want dictates, to a great extent, the size of the overall project. All projects—large and small and everything in between—require the proper materials for their effective construction. In the next chapter, we'll consider the most common building blocks available for you to fashion the retirement package that's best for you.

The Scarborough Plan
1. **Define in detail your retirement lifestyle.**
2. **Calculate exactly how much you'll need in your retirement account.**
3. **Determine how long it will be before you must tap into your retirement assets.**
4. **Start saving the required amounts now.**

THE BUILDING BLOCKS OF YOUR RETIREMENT

Deborah and Gregory, both in their early forties, arrived precisely at 9 A.M. for their appointment. She deposited her Gucci bag on the corner of my desk, and they took their seats. They already had a pretty good idea of their future lifestyle and what it would cost them.

"We'd like some advice about retirement planning," Gregory said.

I said, "Let's start with what you have available."

Gregory detailed their assets: his 401(k) allocated fifty-fifty in stock and bond funds, their savings account, some gold bullion ("my hedge against inflation"), and a big house. And he's counting on a big inheritance from his father.

"I've just started a new job, too," Deborah chimed in "and I wonder if I should join my company's 401(k) plan."

"Look," I said to them, "you have a variety of assets. But you haven't integrated them into a sound retirement plan, and the assets you have may not be appropriate for your needs."

This book focuses on using your 401(k) as the primary building material for your retirement portfolio. As you'll see, your 401(k) can be the foundation, the walls, the roof, and everything in between. The fact is, though, that many of you will have other building blocks that ought not to be wasted. Some of those building blocks you pay for, others you get free. However they arrive at your building site, your job is to see that those materials get incorporated into your retirement building project in a way that enhances, rather than weakens, the entire structure.

That's where this chapter comes in. Instead of getting into the details of every conceivable building block in the financial universe, we will consider the main elements of your retirement portfolio and how each fits into the overall plan. Let's begin with a discussion of the time-honored concept of the "three-legged stool" which financial advisors have been talking about for generations.

The (Formerly) Three-Legged Stool

When I started out in this business, I—like everybody else—told my clients about the three-legged stool. "Think of your retirement as a three-legged stool," I had been taught to say. "One leg is your Social Security entitlement; the second leg is your company-paid pension plan; and the third leg is your own portfolio of savings and investments." Back then, most people could count on all three legs holding up their retirement stool for the balance of their lives. The three-legged stool concept was great — thirty years ago. But by the time most readers of this book retire, the three-legged stool may look more like a unicycle.

Times have changed. The Social Security system is rocky at best. Every month brings a new warning about how Social Security will be bankrupt within a decade or two, about the time that the baby boomers come up for retirement benefits. If nothing else changes, the system will be paying out more than it takes in within the next dozen years. Yet many employers—maybe yours—and financial advisors are warning employees not to count on their Social Security benefits to provide a substantial source of income during their retirement.

Lawmakers have already initiated several changes in

Social Security that will diminish the value of what we eventually get back. For one thing, we'll get it back later than our parents will. Normal retirement age is already on the way up from sixty-five to sixty-seven. Remember the time value of money we mentioned in Chapter 1? Here's where it comes back to bite us. Delaying the payback of what we've paid into Social Security gives inflation that much more time to diminish the value of every dollar we get back.

Current retirees who earn a sizeable income already pay taxes on their Social Security benefits. There's no doubt that you and I would pay more if both thresholds fall and tax rates rise. Obviously, more taxes mean less take-home pay, less money to pay the bills.

Political pressures from retirees present and future will most certainly keep Social Security alive to some extent—even if it's only on life support. Your best bet is not to count on the Social Security leg holding up its share of your retirement stool.

Leg two: your company's pension plan. We'll discuss pension plans in some detail later in this chapter. Here's what you need to understand at this point: companies have been sawing away on this leg of your retirement since the 1980s, when a variety of legislative and regulatory changes made it a nightmare to administer. In 1990, eight pension plans were eliminated for every one that was created. By 1993, companies were terminating 7,000 plans annually and creating only 500. You'll read that companies were simply converting their pension plans to defined contribution plans—like 401(k) plans—but the evidence is not all that encouraging. In that same year—1993—only 12,000 such plans were initiated, while 8,000 were eliminated. And even with the availability of alternative plans, employees like you were participating at rates that remained stagnant throughout the decade.

Count yourself lucky if your company offers you a pension plan (they'll call it a defined benefit plan), and take all they offer you. But don't count your pension dollars just yet, for two reasons. First, as companies go, so go their pension plans. Thanks to legislation like the Employee Retirement Income Security Act (ERISA), it's extremely unlikely that money your company has promised you will be lost to bad investment decisions or fraud. In fact, ERISA established the Pension Benefit Guaranty Corporation to insure pensions in defined benefit plans. On the other hand, there's no guarantee your company will continue its plan. And if your company goes out of business, you may never reach the tenure needed to realize the level of benefits you anticipated. So beware. Think of your pension plan as icing on your retirement cake.

Second, your pension plan almost certainly depends upon decisions you make about sticking with the company. Before you can count on any of that money, you'll have to spend a predetermined number of years with the company. Most likely, the amount of money (as a percentage of your income) will depend upon the total number of (usually consecutive) years you work for the company. That all sounds great until you realize this: the average amount of time anybody spends with one company nowadays is only around five years. Would you actually stay at a job you hate for twenty or thirty years just to get your piece of the pension plan? Well, I sure wouldn't.

The good news is that many companies do offer 401(k) plans as their replacement for the old defined benefit plan. Good news, because you have more control over your 401(k) plan than you'd ever have over a pension plan. Good news, because you won't have to stay with a job you hate just to be able to realize the profits of your 401(k). And good news, because otherwise you'd have no reason to read my book.

Other companies are converting their pension plans to "cash balance" plans which combine some of the features of defined benefit plans (pensions) and defined contribution plans such as 401(k)s. The employer still makes all contributions to the plan and bears the investment risks, but the plan is portable. When you leave the company, rather than losing your benefits, you can typically take a lump-sum distribution for a rollover IRA (which we'll discuss later). These hybrid plans no longer punish workers who change jobs, but they do highlight the need to consult a financial advisor to understand the implications of what you're doing.

What about the third leg of your retirement stool: personal savings? Personal savings includes savings accounts, certificates of deposit (CDs—not the musical or software sort), individual stocks and bonds, life insurance, individual retirement accounts (IRAs), mutual funds, real estate, life insurance, annuities, and the like. We'll discuss most of these assets later in this chapter.

In light of the deficiencies in the other two legs of your stool, personal savings take on greater importance than in the past. Now national savings rates have edged back up to around 5% of income, but they still misrepresent reality. I don't think this means necessarily that people are spending their assets. I think, instead, that a lot of these "lost" savings are actually being funneled into 401(k) accounts, where they are invisible to government statisticians. Still, it points out that—on average—your personal savings (counting your 401(k) account) will need to represent an increasing share of your retirement assets.

Especially with the uncertainty surrounding Social Security and the diminishing availability of company-sponsored retirement plans, you need to find ways of saving a greater proportion of your income. Among the assets mentioned above, your IRA is one of the best places—outside your 401(k)—to protect your retirement savings from both Uncle Sam and yourself until you're ready to start using the income to fund your retirement years. IRAs are so important that I've included a separate chapter on them (Chapter 6). Depending upon the goals you set in Chapter 1, you'll likely need to rely on additional personal savings assets to prepare fully for your retirement years. This is because there are limits to how much of your income you can set aside in IRAs and 401(k)s. Take a look at your budget before you go much farther in your planning process to determine how much more you can put away each month into personal savings.

Before we get into a description of the building blocks of your retirement planning, let's look at one of the main reasons for investing in 401(k) plans, IRAs, and variable annuities: taxes.

Protecting Your Money from Uncle Sam—Legally

First, we need to make a distinction between qualified retirement plans and non-qualified retirement plans. Qualified retirement plans include defined benefit plans ("pension plans") and defined contribution plans, such as the 401(k), 403(b), and profit-sharing plans. These plans "qualify" for various tax advantages by satisfying the relevant provisions of the Internal Revenue Code. For all the money you invest pre-tax into a qualified plan (and all the money *that* money earns), you won't pay taxes until you begin making withdrawals (they call it "taking distributions") years down the road.

Non-qualified retirement plans, formal and informal, include all the rest. They do not receive the same protection against income taxes. Income is invested into such plans post-tax—that is, after you have already paid tax on the money invested. On top of that, you'll also be taxed on the earnings of those investments. Personal savings suffer the same fate as non-qualified plans—they represent post-tax dollars, and their earnings (interest, dividends, and capital gains) get taxed each year.

One of your goals must be to avoid those taxes for as long as legally possible. Why? Because you'll be able to build your retirement package bigger and faster by using every penny right from the start. Let's look at one example of how qualified retirement plans enable your investment to grow much faster than non-qualified retirement plans or personal savings.

Say you have $2,000 to put aside each year. For the purposes of this example, we'll assume that you're in the 28% federal income tax bracket and the 5% income tax bracket for your state. We'll also assume that we've found an investment that will return 7.5% year in and year out for the foreseeable future. This represents a conservative estimate, given the long-term average annual return of 8.5% provided by stocks. Take a look at the difference in value reached by money invested pre-tax in a qualified plan, compared to investments that don't offer deferred taxation. It should be clear that qualified plans—simply by avoiding taxes—out run normally taxed income in no time.

Real Rate of Return

At the end of year	Your qualified plan will have	Your taxed plan will have	A difference of
1	$ 2,150	$ 1,407	$ 743
2	$ 4,461	$ 2,885	$ 1,576
5	$ 12,488	$ 7,780	$ 4,708
10	$ 30,416	$17,722	$ 12,694
15	$ 56,154	$30,425	$ 25,729
20	$ 93,105	$46,658	$ 46,447
25	$146,152	$67,400	$ 78,752
30	$222,309	$93,904	$128,405

And these figures don't take into account the fact that many employers match some of your investment with a contribution of their own into your qualified plan—a match that also grows tax-deferred!

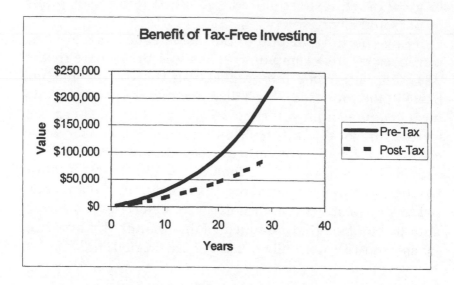

You should be able to take home two messages from this example:

+ First, invest as much as you are permitted within the plan limits into your qualified retirement plan in order to maximize your retirement account's growth and ultimate value.
+ Second, so far as possible, make your own investments first in vehicles such as IRAs which provide the same tax advantages. Your money will grow much faster.

Now that we've covered the important general information, let's examine each of the building blocks of your retirement in some detail. After a brief additional word about Social Security, we'll consider three types of building materials: employee benefit plans, individual retirement accounts, and other assets.

How Social Security Works—or Doesn't—for You

The entire Social Security system aims to provide retirement benefits based on the average worker. Using 1998 figures, Social Security is designed to replace about 40 %

(around $10,000) of the average worker's annual earnings (around $25,000). So if you earned the average income and if Social Security remains viable throughout your retirement, you can count on about $10,000 a year (if you're single; around $16,500 for couples) from Social Security during your retirement years.

If your income is higher than that, however, Social Security will replace a diminishing amount of your annual income. The maximum income on which Social Security tax was paid in 2000 was $76,200. If that's exactly what you earned, you'll receive about $16,500 in retirement benefits, which represents less than a quarter of your pre-retirement income. And since $16,500 is where the payments max out, you can simply do the math to figure out how much of your pre-retirement income will be covered by Social Security payments for other income levels. If you make $100,000 now, you'll realize only 16% of that from Social Security.

The message is clear: the more you earn, the more important it becomes for you to find additional building blocks for your retirement account. In fact, no matter what your income now, you're not going to be able to live on Social Security. As I already explained in Chapter 1, count on spending after retirement what you spend now—not 40% or 25% or 16%, but 100%.

Other changes are in store for Social Security, among them the age at which you'll be allowed to start receiving full benefits. If you were born before 1938, you'll still be able to retire at age sixty-five and begin receiving Social Security payments. But if you were born in later years, you'll have to reach a more advanced age before full payments begin. The schedule currently in place ups the retirement age in two-month increments per year, to a maximum retirement age of sixty-seven years for those of you born in 1960 or later. And don't be surprised if this age grows even older as you get closer to retirement.

Remember, too, that if you plan to work after you retire, you'll earn special penalties for being a hard worker. Currently, the penalty for those aged sixty-five to sixty-nine years old is a one-dollar reduction in Social Security benefits for every three dollars earned in excess of $17,000. The only good news here is that the maximum allowable earnings schedule is also increasing: it's slated to double to around $30,000 by 2002. In fact, legislation has been passed eliminating this penalty altogether, and the President is expected to sign it. Regardless of what happens, once you reach age seventy, the penalties disappear if you continue working. On the other hand, if you continue working past age sixty-five and do not draw benefits until you actually retire, you accumulate Delayed Retirement Credits, which increase your benefits.

Rather than wait another twenty years to find out what Social Security might do for your retirement, it's worth checking to see where your account stands now. Not only will this assist in your retirement planning, but also you'll be able to check your information for accuracy.

Request a Form SSA-7004 (Personal Earnings and Benefits Estimate Statement, or PEBES) by phoning the Social Security Administration at 1-800-772-1213. You can also fill out the form at their web site (www.ssa.gov). In a month or so, you'll receive a report that details your earnings history, your contributions to Social Security, your estimated retirement benefit, and other information about what would happen to your benefits were you to become disabled or to die.

But if you're willing to wait a while, you'll automatically receive statements from the Social Security Administration annually (if you're over age twenty-five years old and not receiving benefits). Of course, you'll need to review these reports, as they may not match your own estimates of future income. These reports should arrive about three months before your birthday—sort of Uncle Sam's way of saying, "Have a happy. . . ."

Retirement Building Blocks from Your Employer

Many—if not most—employers offer some plan for protecting your retirement dollars from current taxes. Your job is to identify these plans and take full advantage of them. Among the most popular employee benefits are the following: pension plans (now called defined benefit plans); 401(k) plans, 403(b) plans, and 457 plans (defined contribution plans); stock options; stock purchase plans; and employee stock ownership plans. Let's consider each of these in turn.

Defined Benefit Plans

Defined benefit pension plans promise employees a specific monthly benefit at retirement. A common trust generally pays benefits according to a formula based on the number of years the employee worked for the company. For example, the benefit may be a certain dollar amount for each year of service (for example, $25 per month at retirement for each month you worked for the company). It could be calculated as a percentage of the employee's salary times the number of years of service (for instance, 1% of your final salary times the number of years you worked), or it may be an exact dollar amount (say, $150 per month at retirement, regardless of your income or term of service).

The employer carries the responsibility for prudently managing the investment of these assets and for paying all the benefits earned by the employee either from the trust or, if the trust has insufficient funds, from the company's own assets.

If both sources become exhausted, the Pension Benefit Guaranty Corporation (PBGC) steps in to cover benefits up to a guaranteed level. The maximum benefit PBGC can pay is set by law each year, and it does not cover things like health and welfare benefits, vacation pay, or certain death benefits. All that being said, about 85% of all participants in plans taken over by PBGC have received all of their earned benefits.

Defined benefit plans offer several advantages to employees of companies that offer them. First, the benefits are predictable. Employees know in advance what benefits are promised them at retirement, so they don't have to worry about the ups and downs of the economy. Furthermore, the benefits depend upon contributions made by the employer, so they don't rely on the ability of the employee to contribute.

Second, the benefits are reasonably secure, guaranteed as they are by the Pension Benefit Guaranty Corporation. If your company folds or cannot afford to pay your benefits, you'll receive all of your earned benefit in most cases.

Finally, defined benefit plans must offer to pay you an annuity—a yearly benefit—throughout your retirement, no matter how long you live. And, unless you and your spouse decide otherwise, the defined benefit plan must also pay a lifelong annuity to your spouse if you die first.

Some defined benefit plans feature other benefits, including early retirement benefits, extra benefits for spouses, disability benefits, or cost-of-living adjustments. Your human resources department can tell you about such value-added features of your pension plan—if your company has one.

401(k) Plans

We'll spend a big part of the rest of the book discussing 401(k) plans. The point in including them here is to distinguish them from defined benefit plans.

401(k) plans fall into the group of qualified retirement plans known as defined contribution plans. In a defined contribution plan, the employee owns the account and, in most cases, directs the investment of the assets in the account. In most cases, both the employee and the employer make regular contributions to the account, with the employer matching employee contributions up to some predetermined percentage of the employee's income. As with defined benefit plans, defined contribution plans are protected from taxes on both the contributions to and the earnings on the account until the employee begins to withdraw funds, usually at retirement. While the amount of pre-tax dollars you contribute to your 401(k) has legal limits, some plans also allow after-tax contributions, though few employees need to take advantage of this feature.

With defined contribution plans, the amount of funds available at retirement depends upon both the contributions of the employee and employer and the earnings realized by the investments. Consequently, defined contribution plans are subject to the vagaries of the economy and the markets. For this reason, wise management of the plan is critical to maximizing the value of your ultimate retirement package. And that's why understanding The Scarborough Plan as described in this book is so important to your financial future. Failing to implement the Plan can result in your retirement account's failing to keep pace with inflation and failing to earn the returns necessary for you to attain your financial goals.

Defined contribution plans offer several additional advantages over some defined benefit plans. Principal among them is their widespread availability. Because of their administrative simplicity and reasonable maintenance cost, plans like the 401(k) plan can be offered by most employers.

Portability represents another significant advantage. Unlike many defined benefit plans, defined contribution plans virtually always offer the possibility of being taken with you when you change jobs—either by depositing the proceeds into a rollover IRA account or by transferring the assets to the 401(k) of your next employer. Even if you leave the account with your former employer, you still own the account. This advantage reduces the problem of vesting—having to work for an employer for a predetermined period—before owning your retirement account, thereby making it easier for you to change jobs throughout your career and still achieve the benefits of tax-protected retirement investing. Vesting may still affect the employer's contributed portion, however.

As an incentive for employees to stay, many large companies have very attractive matching programs. Leaving before you're fully vested could put a dent in your retirement dollars. You need to know the numbers and—with your investment advisor—weigh all the variables carefully when deciding to switch companies before you're fully vested.

Finally, defined contribution plans have slightly outperformed defined benefit plans historically. For the five-year period ending December 31, 1994, defined contribution plans earned an average 10.6% annual rate of return, with an inflation-adjusted real rate of return of 6.8%. During the same period, defined benefit plans averaged 9.8% annually, with an after-inflation return of 6.0%.

This won't be the last time you hear this advice here: if your company offers a 401(k) plan, participate in it as soon as you can, to the fullest extent that you can afford. The 401(k) is the most important building block in your retirement package. Period.

403(b) and 457 Plans

Even though most people reading this book probably won't qualify for these two plans, we'll mention them briefly for completeness. Both plans represent variations on the defined contribution plan theme.

403(b) plans are available through payroll deduction only to employees of certain not-for-profit tax-exempt corporations defined by section 501(c)(3) of the Internal Revenue Code. They include, among others, hospitals, schools, charitable organizations, museums, colleges and universities, and social welfare agencies. The money deducted must be invested in mutual funds, variable annuities, or fixed annuities—but not individual stocks and other options available in 401(k) plans. As with 401(k) plans, contributions may be made by the employee and/or by the employer, though some plans get funded solely by employee contributions.

As of 2000, employees can contribute up to the lesser of $10,500 or the "exclusion allowance," which approximates 20% of includible compensation into these plans, with a catch-up provision for some participants who enter the plan later in their employment. The employee owns the account and may be able to move its funds among the various investment choices free of cost or tax consequences. Some 403(b) plans also offer loan provisions and guaranteed death benefits.

Like 401(k) plans, 403(b) plans can protect the contributions to the plan from taxes. Furthermore, all capital gains, dividends, and interest income accrue tax-deferred until the participant begins to withdraw funds. Retirees can begin to withdraw funds beginning at age 59½ and must begin withdrawing funds by April 1 of the year after the year they turn 70½, unless they are still working, in which case mandatory withdrawals can be deferred indefinitely. Earlier withdrawals will cost you. Unless you retire after age fifty-five, you'll pay normal income taxes on any money you receive, plus a hefty 10% penalty tax, though you might avoid the latter if you can meet the IRS's definition of disability.

Funds in 403(b) accounts are portable, too. Should you leave or retire from the institution that offered the plan, you can move the funds into your Rollover IRA or into a mutual fund or variable annuity that protects the tax-deferral advantages of the 403(b). In fact, if you put money into the plan from salary reduction and the employer did not make contributions for your account, then you can move the 403(b) assets wherever you want without the employer's approval (subject to the penalties mentioned above, if you choose not to move the assets to a qualifying plan). This option proves useful when limited investment choices are offered, when the plan performance is poor, or when there are restrictions about switching within the investment vehicles offered.

The 457 plan—governed by section 457 of the Internal Revenue Code—is a non-qualified (non-qualified means, unfortunately, that the plans are unfunded, unregulated, and don't qualify for favorable tax treatment), deferred compensation plan for states, counties, cities, government agencies, and their political subdivisions. This plan is an unsecured promise by the organization to the employee to defer the employee's compensation to some future date by accepting contributions through salary deduction. Unlike 403(b) and 401(k) plans, no direct ownership of the assets accrues to the employee. Everything relies on the contract between the employee and the institution.

If your company offers a 401(k) or 403(b)plan, participate in it as soon as you can, to the fullest extent that you can afford. It is the most important building block in your retirement package. Period.

Contributions to 457 plans are tax-deductible up to the maximum of $8,000 annually or one-third of the employee's salary, whichever is less. Growth of the funds within the plan is also protected from taxes until they are distributed to the employee. Distributions from 457 plans can be made at retirement, termination of employment, or under extreme financial hardship, as well as to beneficiaries if the employee dies before reaching the other milestones. The distributions cannot be transferred to a rollover IRA, and all payments are taxed as ordinary income. On the other hand, 457 distributions are not subject to the

10% penalty tax imposed on early distributions.

Overall, the 457 plan carries risks that make it less desirable than the other, qualified defined contribution plans. First, you're investing only your own money, so there's no growth realized from a match by the employer. Second, you have no guarantee that the money will be there when you need it. The money you contribute can be taken by the organization's creditors or even by the organization itself. Third, when you retire before age sixty, the funds in the account are distributed and taxed immediately. Before you accept any participation in a 457 plan, be sure you understand all these risks.

Stock Options

While stock options were historically offered to key employees as an incentive to stimulate their efforts to make the company profitable and to remain employed by the company, many firms—particularly young, rapidly growing companies—now offer stock options to the majority of their employees as part of the overall compensation package. Chances are increasingly good that you work for one of those companies or someday will.

Here's how stock options work. The company grants you the right (but not an obligation) to purchase a specified number of shares of the company's stock for an established price within a set period of time. The number of shares for which the right is granted often depends upon such things as your tenure as an employee and your perceived value to the firm. The established price—called an exercise price or strike price—usually reflects the actual market price of the stock near the date your option was granted to avoid certain nasty tax consequences. The period during which your option can be exercised can vary widely. In most cases, stock option agreements also specify vesting schedules that indicate how much of the option you'll be able to exercise when.

Okay, it's not as complicated as it sounds. Consider

this example. You've just received a stock option agreement (sign it and return it after you read it) that says you are granted the option of purchasing 1,000 shares of company stock for $10 a share. You notice right off that the exercise price ($10) is close to yesterday's closing market price of 9¾. The agreement says that you have ten years to exercise the option, so long as you continue working for the company, and that you'll be able to exercise up to 20% of the options in one year, 40% in two years, and so on up to 100% in five years. This is called a vesting schedule. If you leave the company without having exercised the options, you're out of luck (unless you retire, it says, in which case you have one year to exercise whatever options are vested).

Two years from now you get an offer you can't refuse from a rival company. Just before you give notice, you exercise your option to purchase 400 shares of company stock (that's 40% of 1,000) and fork over the $4,000. As luck would have it, the market price of company stock then has reached $17, providing you a nice gain of $2,800. Of course, you could hold the 400 shares of stock and hope for the best, but chances are you'll invest the proceeds elsewhere. The company won't do nearly as well without you around.

By the way, what happens tax-wise when you exercise your options depends upon the type of stock option plan that provided them. With non-qualified stock option plans (NQSOs), you are taxed at your ordinary tax rate on the difference between the exercise price and the market price when you exercise the options, regardless of whether you sell the stock. In the example above, you will be liable for ordinary taxes on that $2,800 difference even if you hold the shares in your portfolio. Should you keep the shares for another year, then you'll pay capital gains tax on the appreciation in value since the date of exercise.

With incentive stock options (ISOs), on the other hand, you pay no ordinary tax at the time you exercise them. Instead, you will be taxed at the long-term capital gains rate so long as you hold the stock for at least two years from the date the option was granted and one year from the date the option was exercised. This can result in a substantial tax savings if your ordinary tax rate differs significantly from the (current) 20% long-term capital gains tax rate.

Stock options cost you nothing, and they carry potentially unlimited value. Take them if your company offers them. But read your stock option agreements closely. Especially important are the vesting schedules and the rules regarding the exercise of the options when you decide to leave or retire. You'd hate to lose thousands of dollars in potential retirement funds by doing something stupid, like trying to exercise the options after they've expired.

Stock Purchase Plans

Stock purchase plans enable employees to buy company stock through payroll deductions, often at prices discounted from existing market prices. Though this could provide you with an immediate capital gain (because of the difference between the market price and your discounted price), you face no tax consequences until you actually sell the stock. Especially if you have faith in your company's future prospects, this is a great way to amass large amounts of company stock over a period of time. Even if you harbor little hope of long-term profitability for your company, there's no reason not to take advantage of the gift provided by the discount your company offers.

Whether or not you participate in the stock purchase plan may depend on factors more political than financial. Will your company look askance at you if you buy discounted stock only to sell it the same day for a profit? Will such behavior brand you as disloyal or "not a team player?" These are the real considerations, not the financial factors. This one's a no-brainer: buy something for less than it's worth, sell it for what it's worth, and keep the difference (well, after you pay ordinary taxes on the profit). If it doesn't affect how you're perceived by your company, why would you not do this?

Employee Stock Ownership Plans (ESOPs)

ESOPs and stock bonus plans resemble other qualified profit sharing plans. The only difference is that all the funds are invested in company stock. The great thing about ESOPs is the favorable tax treatment they receive. When you receive a distribution of stock from your ESOP (or stock bonus plan), you are taxed on what the plan paid for the stock, but not on the unrealized appreciation of the stock unless you choose to be taxed at that point. *Choose to be taxed?* you ask. Believe it or not, yes. If, at that point, your ordinary tax rate was less than the prevailing capital gains tax rate, you'd save money by paying taxes then at the lower rate, especially if you expected your ordinary tax rate later to be higher than the capital gains rate.

Instead, when you sell the stock, your gain (the difference between what you sell the stock for and what the plan bought the stock for) would be taxable as long-term capital gains, subject to a maximum tax rate of 20%. This way you defer the tax and (depending upon your ordinary tax rate) pay a lower tax rate that you ordinarily would.

Here's another special tax feature of ESOPs that benefits your heirs. If you die, they will pay income tax (but not till they sell the stock) on the unrealized appreciation between the price your ESOP paid for the stock and the value of the stock when it was distributed to you (not the appreciation between the distribution and the date they sell it). Great deal for them, but it doesn't help you a bit.

ESOPs can be rolled over into an IRA, but they lose their favorable tax treatment at that point. Instead of being taxed at the capital gains rate when withdrawn from your IRA, the funds will be taxed at your ordinary income tax rate upon withdrawal.

Retirement Building Blocks You Make Yourself

You needn't rely on your employer for everything in your retirement package. In fact, you need to do some building on your own if you expect to reach your retirement financial goals. Current allowable limits for contributions to pension plans and 401(k) plans and the like make it virtually certain that you'll have to collect other building blocks to bolster your retirement package. Some of your investment—but not much—should be in the form of cash and things like cash. These assets provide no tax advantages and offer returns so low that you have them because you must, not because you want them (in that form). Your main efforts in this arena should be directed toward building your individual retirement accounts (IRAs), the only building blocks here that protect you from the onslaught of taxation and inflation.

Cash

By cash, I mean *invested* cash, not cash stuffed in mattresses or sewn into the lining of overcoats or piled up in your attic. Except for what you have in your pocket or purse, you should have no cash that isn't actively working for you, earning interest income however small. No, by cash, I mean money in savings accounts, money market funds, or certificates of deposit.

You need some cash set aside for meeting your regular living expenses and for dealing with unexpected events that inevitably arise. How much? Not much. Besides having cash for your monthly budget, you should probably have additional cash amounting to three to six months' worth of living expenses, depending on your own personal situation. This should enable you to deal with most reasonably likely contingencies. Beyond that much cash, you're probably not letting your assets work efficiently for you.

Take a look at your next bank statement and you'll realize what has been true historically. Investments in cash have yielded returns that only slightly exceed inflation, and that's before taxes. When you add taxes into the mix, your savings account, interest-bearing checking account, money market funds, and certificates of deposit probably lose purchasing power every minute they sit there.

What's an investor to do? Recognize the facts and try to minimize—to the extent you can do so safely—the amount of your wealth you keep as cash. Cash loses value more quickly than any other financial instrument, over the long haul. Keep only what you need and invest the rest in something that provides better returns.

Individual Retirement Accounts (IRAs)

IRAs deserve more detailed treatment than the other building blocks, so I've given them their own chapter (Chapter 6). Still, it's worthwhile mentioning here why you should consider investing what might otherwise sit around as cash in one of the available types of IRA. Tax protection stands out as the main reason—but you know that by now.

You may not want to choose an IRA over a 401(k) plan as your main retirement investment, but you can use an IRA to complement your retirement package. Under the following conditions you can make contributions both to an IRA and to your 401(k) plan and realize tax deductions on the entire amount:

- You are single and earn less than $32,000 a year
- You are married, file a joint return, and earn less than $52,000 a year (you and your spouse combined)

And if you satisfy these conditions, you can deduct a portion of the amount invested in your IRA:

- You are single and earn between $32,000 and $42,000 a year
- You are married, file a joint return, and you earn between $52,000 and $62,000 a year (with your spouse)

If you earn more than these amounts, you are still able to make contributions to a nondeductible IRA and you might qualify for a contribution to a Roth IRA, but you can never exceed the maximum annual IRA contribution limit of $2,000 ($4,000 for couples). Note also that the deduction thresholds will rise over the next several years to $50,000-$60,000 for single individuals by 2005 and to $80,000-$100,000 for couples by 2007.

If neither you nor your spouse participate in a qualified retirement plan, you can make the maximum deductible contribution to your IRA regardless of your income.

Roth IRAs offer some features not provided by regular IRAs. Principal among the benefits is the unprecedented tax advantage. Dividends, interest, and capital gains within a Roth IRA are not taxable, and monies distributed are received tax-free so long as the account has been owned for at least 5 years and the owner is at least 59½ years old.

The Roth IRA is subject to a whole set of income limitations that I'll discuss in Chapter 6. Your best bet is to ask your accountant or financial advisor whether and to what extent you qualify for a Roth IRA. For many people, the Roth IRA will prove better than the traditional IRA as a retirement building block.

Retirement Building Blocks from Your Other Assets

When you're figuring out how to finance your retirement years, don't lose sight of the other investments you've managed to accumulate over a lifetime of financial planning. Many of these assets do not provide the tax protection afforded by such investments as IRAs and 401(k) plans, but prudent management can provide considerable wealth that will enable you to delay withdrawals from your tax-protected accounts.

What are some of these assets? Let's discuss four: your portfolio of investments, insurance, annuities, and inheritances and other lotteries.

Your Portfolio

Besides the money you put away intending to use it during your retirement, you should be investing everything beyond the cash reserve we mentioned above in assets that generate a healthy return at an acceptable level of risk. These investments should be concentrated in stocks, bonds, or tax-efficient or tax-appropriate mutual funds. How you divide your funds among these investments depends upon principles I'll discuss in Chapter 3 (asset allocation), but you'll realize the highest returns for any given level of risk by appropriately spreading your investment dollars among a variety of instruments.

Stocks have historically earned greater returns than other investments. If you have time to do some research and know something about what you're doing, you can divide the dollars you invest in stock among at least 15 different companies in various industry or market sectors. This diversification may help protect you against unexpected events affecting individual companies, providing you an equivalent return at a lower level of risk. All other things being equal, the more individual stocks you own, the less volatile your overall portfolio may be.

However, I don't think most people have the time or the expertise to be successful at managing a portfolio of individual stocks. Instead, I strongly advise clients to invest in mutual funds. Not one mutual fund, but several mutual funds to provide you an assortment of investment classes—big companies, small companies, foreign companies, and so on.

Remember, too, that I'm talking investing, not timing. For most of your life, most of your investments should be in stock mutual funds. The only thing I can absolutely guarantee you about timing the market—that is, guessing when the market's moving up and when it's moving down—is that it rarely works. You will inevitably be out of the market during times when you could be earning gains, and, if you're like most individual investors, you'll find yourself buying near the top of the market and selling near the bottom. Regardless of whether you're investing for retirement or investing for higher living, my advice to you is this: buy stock mutual funds and keep them. Don't try to time the market. You'll lose.

Bonds make up the next significant class of assets in your portfolio. With bonds, you are, in effect, lending money to someone else in exchange for a regular return on your loan. That someone else may be the government—who pays you somewhat less, but offers you as close to a risk-free investment as you'll find, with the added feature of earnings that are free of state and federal taxes—or it may be a company. Similar benefits arise from TIPS (Treasury inflation-protected securities) and municipal bonds. If you opt for corporate bonds, be sure you understand bond ratings or know someone who does. Just because a company offers a bond paying 18% doesn't mean you want to have it in your portfolio. That company—and its bonds—may be pure junk.

The simple reason that you want less of your money invested in bonds than you have invested in stock is this: over virtually every period in recent financial history, bonds provide returns below those provided by stocks. Over the course of most of the twentieth century, bonds have provided earnings about four percentage points less than stocks, even taking taxes and transaction fees into account. Equities consistently outpace taxes and inflation over time, thereby preserving your purchasing power.

Nevertheless, bonds form an important component of your personal and retirement portfolio. Because their returns tend to move in directions opposite stocks, they provide the same benefits as diversification—that is, they help to sustain your overall portfolio growth at a lower overall risk. In effect, they may provide protection against wide swings in the stock market by swinging in the opposite direction. Later in life, as steady income becomes at least as important as steady growth, bonds grow in importance as the stable income-providing component of your portfolio.

In summary, then, what comprises your personal portfolio as you near retirement will contribute to your retirement cash flow and enable you to perpetuate the tax-protection of your retirement assets even longer. Whether you choose individual stocks and bonds or stock and bond mutual funds, you will want your portfolio to contain both types of instruments. You'll learn how (and why) to allocate your monies among those instruments in the next chapter.

Insurance

Insurance after you retire should be viewed more as protection against spending all your retirement funds rather than as a source of retirement funds. For that reason, you may want to have health insurance, long-term care insurance, and property and liability insurance. You might even want life insurance, for reasons I'll mention below.

Medical care doesn't come cheap. And Medicare doesn't cover everything. For these two reasons alone, you need additional health insurance. The fortunate among you will be able to continue your employer's health insurance coverage after you retire. Those of you who can't should explore the various insurance plans that supplement Medicare. Here are just a few costs not covered by Medicare: skilled nursing home care (after the first 100 days), custodial care (someone to watch over you), most prescription drugs, and any medical care you need when you're abroad. Supplemental health insurance—so-called Medigap insurance—can be purchased to cover many of these costs.

Long-term care insurance covers such expenses as skilled nursing care, custodial care, intermediate care (some nursing and rehabilitative services), and some home health care. While decisions about whether to purchase this fairly pricey insurance will depend upon your personal health and family history, the statistics say it may be a worthwhile investment, especially for those who disdain public assistance. The longer you live, the greater your chances of requiring long-term institutionalization—at costs ranging to $50,000 a year and beyond.

Property and liability insurance makes sense after retirement for the same reason it makes sense before retirement. Bad things happen. Lightning strikes, trees fall, people slip and injure themselves. You don't want to take the next twenty years saving for your retirement and then have to spend it repairing your home or paying somebody else's lawyer for their back injury, right? Right!

And just a few words about life insurance. Let's say you've been less than completely diligent in planning for your retirement. Let's say that your surviving spouse won't have enough money to live on after you're buried or cremated or whatever. Life insurance can be used to make up that gap in income. Especially if you will be relying on Social Security and your pension plan to support you during your retirement, you should consider life insurance. When you die, both benefit payments will probably fall substantially, and the loss of income could prevent your spouse from maintaining the lifestyle you enjoyed together. Life insurance proceeds are frequently used to pay estate taxes, too, which makes them especially valuable for high net-worth individuals. And cash-value insurance plans may be used to satisfy some cash flow requirements at retirement.

Annuities

Annuities are financial instruments you can purchase that promise to pay you a monthly, annual, or lump-sum benefit during your retirement. Insurance companies offer them, as do other financial services companies. A major benefit offered by annuities is the tax-deferral they provide. Withdrawals, when you take them, are taxable at your then-current income tax rate, unless you take a distribution before age 59½, in which case you'll pay the usual IRS ten percent tax penalty, too.

As you might have gathered, I don't favor annuities as first-line financial instruments. Because they do, however, provide the benefit of tax deferral, they can be quite useful for people who don't have the option of participating in 401(k) plans. Variable annuities are certainly part of the mix you should consider with your retirement advisor.

Inheritances and Other Lotteries

The only reason for mentioning these two "assets" is that they may reduce the amount of money you ultimately need to invest in your retirement package. As building blocks, though, they're more like housewarming gifts than brick and mortar. If you get one, great—but don't count on it. Those rich uncles and aunts have a way of falling in love with younger people and needy charities, so those millions you've been expecting may find their way into other people's bank accounts.

And if you're counting those lottery winnings among your retirement dollars, I suggest you start planning to work the rest of your life while you're waiting to cash in the winning ticket. But if you must buy a lottery ticket, and you are one of the very few who actually wins any significant amount of money, take the cash option. Use your cash winnings to invest in stocks and bonds.

How you fit these building blocks together forms the subject of the next chapter. In Chapter 3, you'll learn about asset allocation—why it's important and how to do it. Efficient asset allocation is a major component of The Scarborough Plan for maximizing the power of your 401(k) plan. But knowing how best to allocate your assets will also give you a big advantage in organizing your own investment portfolio. So don't just sit there, read on.

The Scarborough Plan

1. Define in detail your retirement lifestyle.
2. Calculate exactly how much you'll need in your retirement account.

3. Determine how long it will be before you must tap into your retirement assets.

4. Start saving the required amounts now.

5. **Determine your estimated Social Security income.**

6. **After your 401(k), rank your other investments according to the tax advantages they offer.**

7. **Invest your retirement savings in tax-deferred alternatives first.**

3
WHAT YOU NEED TO KNOW ABOUT ASSET ALLOCATION

Toward the back of the seminar room, a tall fellow with a quizzical look in his eyes rose to ask a question. I'd just been talking about my approach to asset allocation.

"You mean," he asked, "my advisor's recommendation to have 100% minus my age in stocks is a crazy idea?"

"It's a cookie-cutter approach," I answered. "It doesn't take your own personal situation into account at all. Besides, it's usually overly-conservative."

After the seminar, I saw him in the lobby, madly pounding the keypad of his cell phone.

I can hear you asking yourself, *Why in the world has Scarborough written a whole chapter on asset allocation?* Well, here's why: because you need to know about it. Proper asset allocation—and the principles associated with it—forms the backbone of The Scarborough Plan. If you want to spread out your investments according to some article written in the *Wall Street Journal* or something you saw on *Wall Street Week,* that's your prerogative. But if you want to use an asset allocation strategy that's designed *uniquely for you,* then you need this chapter.

There's more to asset allocation than simply deciding how to divvy up your investment dollars among the various asset classes. That's another reason for this chapter. Here's what you'll be learning about over the next few pages:

- The importance of starting early
- How dollar cost averaging can lead to above-average returns
- Why management style makes a difference
- The asset types and how they have performed historically
- The risks you encounter along the way
- Something called the Efficient Frontier Model; and
- How The Scarborough Plan makes all these elements work for you.

The Early Bird Gets the Wealth

The age at which you start investing for your retirement makes an enormous difference in the ultimate size of your retirement account. Sure, this seems obvious, but the power of compounding makes the difference much bigger than you might imagine. The difference is not merely the number of years multiplied by the amount invested. Remember that each year's investment also grows by the amount your assets can earn.

Two examples should help you appreciate the difference. First, let's examine what happens to exactly the same annual investment begun at different ages. We'll assume that you start investing $1,000 a year in an IRA or other tax-deferred account that provides you a 7% annual return (note again that we're using a rate well below the 8.5% inflation-adjusted average annual return of stocks). What happens to that investment by the time you reach age sixty-five?

If you start investing when you're	At age 65, you'll have
20	$305,752
25	$213,610
30	$147,913
35	$101,073
40	$ 67,676
45	$ 43,865
50	$ 26,888
55	$ 14,784
60	$ 6,153

Or, to put it graphically:

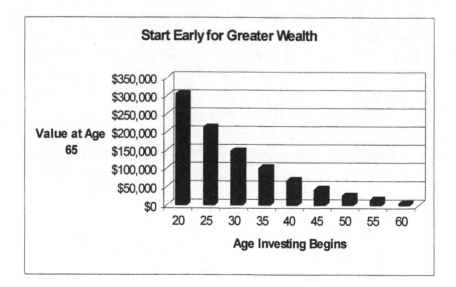

Next, let's look at it from a different perspective. We'll keep the assumptions similar, with one difference. You decide that you want to arrive at age sixty-five with the same retirement account value as if you had begun investing that $1,000 tax-free every year when you were twenty years old. In other words, how much money would you have to invest each year—beginning at the same ages indicated in the previous example—to reach age sixty-five with a portfolio worth $305,752? Here's the answer:

If you start investing when you're	You'll need to invest each year
20	$ 1,000
25	$ 1,532
30	$ 2,211
35	$ 3,237
40	$ 4,834
45	$ 7,458
50	$12,167
55	$22,130
60	$53,167

The graph looks like this:

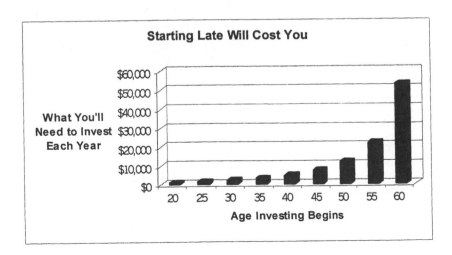

These two examples should provide you sufficient incentive to get your retirement investment plan into gear immediately. Either way you look at it, the earlier you start investing, the more you'll have to work with when the time comes to start using it. The longer you wait, the less you'll have—or the more you'll have to invest to catch up. Better enroll in your company's 401(k) plan today.

Beating the Averages With Dollar Cost Averaging

Dollar cost averaging is a fancy term that means this: investing the same amount of money regularly—weekly, monthly, quarterly—no matter what the market happens to be doing. With most employee benefit plans, including your 401(k) plan, dollar cost averaging occurs automatically. You have a certain amount of your pay deducted each pay period and invested in your 401(k) account. So you are dollar cost averaging whether you knew it or not.

What's so great about dollar cost averaging? It provides a big advantage in spreading out your risk. Whatever stocks or bonds or mutual funds you invest in will vary in price from day to day or, in this case, from pay period to pay period. By investing the same amount of money each time, you will sometimes pay a little more per share, sometimes pay a little less per share. Rather than trying to guess whether or not the price is fair (in other words, whether the time is right to buy)—which I already said pretty much guarantees failure—you'll spend, on the average, less per share over time than those who buy the same shares all at once.

Dollar cost averaging also takes some of the emotions—or foolish decisions, depending on how you look at it—out of investing. When prices rise, you'll be buying fewer shares. When prices fall, you'll be buying more shares. Left to your own devices, you'd probably fall prey to the usual herd mentality—buying when stocks are hot (and prices are high) and selling them when they fall out of favor (and prices are low). Dollar cost averaging keeps you in the market and, over time, may save you money. And in my book, saving money is just as good as making money.

Dollar cost averaging makes such good scnsc that you ought to consider using the same strategy in your personal investing plans. Studies have shown that it can work both to provide you a lower average cost for your investments and to reduce your risk of short-term losses than when you invest everything at once. But, as I said, this is all done for you with your 401(k) plan. You decide how much comes out of your check each pay period, and the rest just happens: automatic dollar cost averaging.

Management Style and Your Money

Management style has nothing to do with what you wear. It has to do with the basic approach to managing an investment portfolio. Investment management style matters, because most components of your 401(k) will be mutual funds, cach run by an individual portfolio manager. As much as those managers would like you to believe that the quality of their funds' performances relate to the skill of the managers, the fact is that the manager's ability to pick the right stocks (or bonds) to buy and sell accounts for only a small portion of the fund's overall performance. Guess what accounts for the bulk of the performance. Exactly! The manager's investment style.

We will consider two sorts of style here. One way to categorize style is according to the way the portfolio itself is managed. Here, the division falls into passive and active management styles.

Passive management means simply that some system determines which stocks constitute the portfolio, so that hands-on management *per se* is not required. The best example of passive management is index funds. Index funds are funds that are designed to mimic the performance of some financial index. An S&P 500 index fund, for example, would include the stocks that make up the Standard & Poor's 500 stock index in amounts reflecting their proportions in the index. Such a fund would require adjustments only as needed to maintain the correct relative amounts of each stock to continue to mirror the S&P 500 index. An S&P 500 index fund, then, should provide investors the same return they would realize from owning each of the individual stocks in the same proportions as the weighted index—or perhaps a bit more or less, depending upon costs and fees encountered. At any rate, the point is this: passive management involves managing the logistics, rather than selecting the stocks that make up the portfolio or fund.

Active management means that the investor—whether an individual investor or a mutual fund portfolio manager— selects which stocks to buy and which stocks to sell according to certain criteria. Actively managed portfolios perform only as well as the stocks that constitute them, so that what the active manager does greatly affects the returns on investments. Active management must combine good stock selection with reasonable turnover—the frequency with which stocks are bought and sold—in order to achieve acceptable returns.

Portfolio management represents a continuum between passive management and active management. As I indicated, index funds live on the passive extreme of this scale. How actively managed other portfolios are may be determined from information provided in the periodic reports from the mutual fund company or from a tracking service like *Morningstar*. Look for the number called turnover. You may find a nominal figure (2.3, for example, would mean that the entire portfolio was changed nearly two and one-third times in the period reported—that's quite a lot) or a percentage figure (30% for example, would mean that 30% of the portfolio from the beginning of the period had been replaced by the end of the period). Turnover gives you a sense of how aggressive the portfolio or fund manager has been in trying to maximize the returns. It also helps explain the transaction fees encountered by the fund.

Another way of dividing style is according to the way "active" investors (or, in this case, portfolio managers) select the stocks they buy. The two main approaches include growth investing and value investing.

Growth investors buy stocks whose earnings are rising rapidly. The companies behind these stocks post strong revenue advances, increasing profitability, and notable competitive advantages over their industry peers. Growth investors invest in these companies because they anticipate continued strong growth, which will be reflected in price appreciation and—for the investor—substantial capital gains. Growth investors have little concern for such things as debt or high price/earnings ratios or other factors that might give other investors pause. They analyze the company, and if they foresee growth, they buy.

Value investors, on the other hand, tend to buy stocks neglected by the rest of the market. They seek companies whose value exceeds that reflected in the stock price. In other words, they attempt to pay less than the stock is worth and then wait for the rest of the market to recognize the company's value and drive the price up. Value investors search for hidden value among corporations that are going through tough times, companies whose value hasn't been recognized by the rest of the market, and companies that are just plain out of favor with investors. The money manager's selection of these companies is based more on the company's management or business strength than on its earnings.

It stands to reason that you ought to know which style a particular mutual fund manager uses in selecting stocks. Contrary to what you might think, the name of the fund does not necessarily reflect the style of the fund manager. Growth funds may be managed by value managers, and vice versa. What's an investor to do? You could watch what the fund is buying and selling yourself—chances are, if the fund is buying stocks with high price/earnings ratios, then it's a growth investor, for example. But you'll find it much easier to consult one of the many mutual fund rating services. *Morningstar*, which I already mentioned, as well as *Standard & Poor's, Lipper, Value Line*, and others, notes the investing style of the fund manager, as well as categorizing funds according to the size of company they tend to buy.

No doubt you're wondering which type of investor—value or growth—fares better over the long run. The simple answer is, they both do—in different markets. The two styles tend to alternate cycles where one style outperforms the other. As usual, the problem here is that the style in favor often isn't clearly identified until well into the other style's cycle. You get around this problem by owning funds that reflect both styles of investing. In other words, besides considering what types of stocks (or mutual funds) need to be in your retirement portfolio, you must also consider what types of investors are choosing those stocks. Given the opportunity, therefore, you'd want a variety of stock mutual funds in your portfolio—at least one managed by a growth-style manager, another managed by a value-style manager.

Asset Classes and Performance

An asset is simply something of value. When the term is used in investing, it refers to the entity in which you are investing your money (which is itself an asset). While assets are commonly divided into stocks and bonds, any sensible discussion of assets and asset allocation requires a finer division of these broad categories. Accordingly, we're going to consider these classes of assets:

- U. S. Treasury bills
- U. S. Treasury bonds
- High grade corporate bonds
- High yield ("junk") corporate bonds
- Growth stocks: large-cap, mid-cap, and small-cap
- Value stocks: large-cap, mid-cap, and small-cap
- Real estate investment trusts
- Precious metals

♦ International bonds
♦ International stocks

Before discussing these asset classes and their per-formance, though, I want to be sure you understand two key terms that I'll be using from here on. The first is *annualized return*. Annualized return represents the percentage return on an investment that would have to be earned each year to explain the total return actually earned over a long period of time. It is not a simple average. Take this simple example. You invest one dollar. The first year, your invest-ment earns 100%, leaving you with two dollars. The sec-ond year, your investment loses 50%, leaving you with one dollar again. Your average annual return—25%—is greatly misleading: it implies that you made something over the two-year period. That's why we won't be using average re-turns. Your annualized return in this example is 0%, which accurately reflects the fact that what you ended up with (one dollar) is just what you'd have if you earned 0% each year for two years.

The second key term is *standard deviation*. Standard deviation is a statistical term that, in our case, measures the chance that what you actually receive in a given year will be close to the annualized return. Standard deviation represents the riskiness of the return. A high standard deviation indicates that a given year's return may miss the annualized return by a wide margin (high or low), while a low standard deviation suggests that each year's return is likely to be close to the annualized return. Because of the way standard deviations are calculated, two-thirds of the time your actual return will fall between one standard de-viation below and one standard deviation above the annu-alized return.

Let's see if an example clarifies this concept. You are considering two investments. Both investments have his-torically provided annualized returns of 10%, but their stan-

dard deviations are quite different. The first investment—
call it Stock Fund A—has a standard deviation of 25%, while
the second investment—Stock Fund B—has a standard
deviation of 5%. How do you translate this into an understanding of their relative risk? Here's one way: over the
next year, both stocks have a 67% chance of missing their
annualized return of 10%. If that happens, then, Stock Fund
A could provide between a 15% loss and a 35% gain, while
Stock Fund B could provide between a 5% gain and a 15%
gain. Stock Fund A is "riskier" because you could miss
your expectations by a wider margin, while Stock Fund B
is less risky because your actual return is likelier to be
close to your expected return.

When you are evaluating assets, both annualized returns and standard deviations provide critical information.
Your objective should always be to maximize your annualized returns within the level of risk (as measured by standard deviation) that you can stomach. Everyone wants high
returns, but not everyone can sleep at night with high levels of risk. And, unfortunately, high returns and high risk
tend to go hand in hand.

To give you some idea of how different assets have
performed over the years, I've tabulated their annualized
returns and standard deviations—as well as the worst one-
year performance—for the two decades spanning 1980
through 1999 below. You should notice immediately how
closely the risks (standard deviations) parallel the returns
(annualized returns).

U. S. Treasury Bills

Treasury bills ("T-bills") are assets issued by the United
States Treasury with maturities of less than one year. Treasury bills are loans: you give Uncle Sam a dollar; he promises to give it back with interest within the year. This is the
safest investment on earth—maybe in the universe. Short
of a complete meltdown of our government, these bills will

1980-1999			
Asset	**Annualized Return**	**Risk** (Stnd Dev)	**Best 1-Yr Return**	**Worst 1-Yr Return**
U. S. Treasury Bills	6.89	2.96	+14.71	+2.90
U. S. Treasury Bonds	9.77	7.54	+27.75	-3.37
High-grade Corporate Bonds	10.53	10.18	+39.21	-3.92
High-yield Corporate Bonds	12.46	12.52	+43.75	-6.38
Large Growth Stocks	17.87	13.10	+37.43	-4.91
Small Growth Stocks	13.96	17.13	+46.05	-19.51
REITs*	9.68	16.86	+36.87	-33.46
International Stocks	14.79	21.45	+69.94	-23.19
Multi-Sector Bonds	9.19	7.44	+21.23	-5.89
Precious Metals	1.91	31.99	+80.29	-41.32

*REIT = Real Estate Investment Trust

never default, so you can count on getting your money back.

Along with their safety comes a paltry return. Over the long term, Treasury bills have provided essentially risk-free returns that barely cover the inflation rate—the annualized returns of Treasury bills over the period between 1926 and 1999 were only 3.69%, with standard deviation of only 3.29%. Small risk, small gain.

U. S. Treasury bonds

Treasury bonds are longer-term loans you grant to the U. S. Treasury. Maturities can range from ten years to thirty years (loans between one and ten years are called Treasury notes). Like T-bills, bonds offer safety of principal value. You will get all your money back (if you hold the bond to maturity), and you will receive regular interest payments during the time the government has your money.

The problem is, you're stuck with that interest rate throughout the duration of the bond. If interest rates rise, the only way you can take advantage of them is to sell your bond (which, because the way the market works, will have a lower principal value in higher interest environments) and buy another one. This way the market has of adjusting the value of your bond's principal can result in losses if you sell the bond early. As a result, one-year returns on twenty-year bonds would have produced losses in sixteen of the past sixty-nine years.

There are two ways of minimizing this risk. The hard way is to purchase twenty-year bonds that mature in different years, giving you a twenty-year bond that matures each year you need the principal back. This is called a laddered maturity. The easy way is to let someone else manage the maturities for you by investing in a U. S. Treasury mutual fund. Unless you have lots of money to buy individual U. S. Treasuries, the second choice is the better bet.

High grade corporate bonds

Companies, like governments, sometimes need money but don't want to ask the bank for it. Instead, they issue bonds. When you buy the bonds, you are lending money to the company.

If you're going to be a lender, you ought to act like one. Check out the ability of the company to repay the money by looking up its bond rating from Standard & Poor's or Moody's Investor Service. The higher the rating, the likelier the company is to pay back the loans. You'll also find that higher bond ratings enable the company to pay lower coupons—lower interest rates—on the money you lend them.

Corporate bonds pay slightly higher yields than do government bonds because of their higher risk. As with government bonds, you'll be stuck with the same interest rate for the duration of the bond, too, so it's important not to buy a single bond of a single company. Again, better to buy a bond mutual fund and let the fund manager spread your risk over a number of bonds from different companies and with different maturities.

High yield ("junk") corporate bonds

High yield corporate bonds pay high yields because they must in order to attract investors. Junk bonds are issued by companies in trouble, companies with little or no track record, and companies with weak balance sheets (that is, lots of debt with little matching equity). Consequently, their bond ratings are low or nonexistent. What you get—if you get it—is the highest interest rate available from corporate bonds. Besides the risks already mentioned above, you also face a substantial risk of default, resulting in the loss of your principal.

Junk bonds are for the highly risk-tolerant investor. Even if you place yourself into that category, cover some of your risks by diversifying—either buy several junk bonds or invest your money in a junk bond mutual fund.

Growth and value stocks

As I mentioned in my discussion of style, the distinction between growth and value stocks lies in the general agreement on their intrinsic value. Growth stocks are recognized as those that offer substantial, long-term growth in their worth, as measured by consistently rising earnings. In general, value stocks, on the other hand, are valued more for their underlying assets than for their current earnings. Many such companies are burdened with substantial debt loads, and value investors or managers select them based on their assessment of the company's potential for using the assets effectively to reap the rewards once they emerge from their debt burden.

Large stocks represent the stocks of America's largest

companies. You'll find the names of these companies in the Fortune 500, the Forbes 400, the Dow Jones averages, and the S&P 500. Unlike bonds, stocks represent ownership in the company. As an owner, you benefit from the company's good times and suffer during the company's bad times.

Profitable, well-run companies gain the market's favor and realize gains in their stock price, enabling you to realize a profit—a capital gain—when you decide to sell the stock. Some such companies pay part of their profits to you as a dividend, but your main interest is the growth of the company's value as reflected in an ever-increasing stock price.

Over the years, large company stocks have fared well—far better than bonds—with inflation-adjusted annualized returns of more than 7%. At this rate, your portfolio value can double nearly every ten years. Of course, your high returns come at a substantial price—the standard deviation of returns over the past seven decades hovers around 20%. In other words, you're equally likely to experience a 13% loss in a year as you are to realize a 27% gain in a year.

In the long run, though, this asset class will give you the best investment value. That's why virtually every advisor with any experience tells you to put some of your investment dollars here. The market swings call for patience, more than anything else, and persistence. Dollar cost averaging combined with investments in stocks gives you the best overall strategy for maximizing your retirement portfolio.

Small stocks, like large company stocks, represent your partial ownership of the company—in this case, a smaller company. Small company doesn't mean your local entrepreneur, though. The term is used to describe those companies whose market value falls below a certain arbitrary value. Depending on whom you ask, "small" could mean the smallest 20% of companies listed on a stock exchange, or it could mean all companies whose market capitalization is less than $1 billion. Market capitalization, or "market cap," cquals the market value of the company's stock. It is determined by multiplying the current price per share of stock times the total number of shares of stock available for trading.

Returns and risks for small growth stocks top the list for U. S. investment classes. Between 1926 and 1999 small stocks provided an annualized return of more than 12%. At the same time, though, the returns were extremely volatile, as reflected in the standard deviation of nearly 35%. Investing solely in small company stocks can take you for quite a roller coaster ride. Later, I'll explain how you can keep some small stocks in your retirement portfolio and still be able to sleep nights.

Medium-sized stocks—or mid-cap stocks—fall between large stocks and small stocks, both in terms of size and returns. Their returns are generally less volatile (or less risky) than those from small stocks, simply because the companies tend to be more established, more experienced, or better managed.

Real estate investment trusts

Real estate investment trusts (REITs) derive their income from commercial property management—property like office buildings and shopping malls. REITs can be purchased like individual stocks or as part of a REIT mutual fund. They can provide returns in excess of those realized by investing in bonds, but at a significantly higher risk.

You'll find REITs among some 401(k) plan options. I mention them because they offer yet another way of reducing the overall risk of your retirement portfolio by providing an added element of diversification.

Precious metals

Precious metals and precious metals stocks represent either gold, platinum, and silver, or the industries that mine them. Many investors flock to the precious metals in times of great economic and political uncertainty. Historically, as you can see from the table, their returns don't justify their risks. Like REITs, precious metals offer only one benefit I can think of—diversification. They should be one of the last places you put your money.

International bonds

Like the U. S. Treasury and U. S. corporations, foreign governments and companies lend money by selling bonds. When purchased as international bonds, these assets can make worthwhile additions to your retirement account. International bonds provide a quality of diversification not afforded by U. S. bonds, for reasons I'll discuss below.

International stocks

International stocks are the foreign equivalent of U. S. stocks. In some cases, they offer greater growth potential than U. S. stocks, though at a greater risk. Foreign stock markets tend to be less regulated and more volatile. They also expose you to currency exchange rate risks and to the risks posed by unpredictable political upheaval abroad. Like international bonds, they can provide a protective diversification, despite their higher risk, and can add to your portfolio's performance. Your 401(k) account's—and your personal portfolio's—performance will benefit from the inclusion of both international stocks and international bonds.

Understanding the Risks

There are no risk-free investments. Period.

Sure, you can invest in Treasury bills and be relatively certain that you'll get back your principal plus the promised interest. But can you be sure that the interest will be greater than the rate of inflation while you were waiting for your money back? No. Can you be certain of getting all your principal back if you need to cash in your T-bill early? Sorry, no. And is there any assurance that you'll be able to get the same interest rate (or higher) on the next Treasury bill you buy? No, none. So when finance types say that Treasury bills are risk-free, what they really mean is that these bills carry almost no credit risk. Practically speaking, though, the interest rate risk over the short-term is small, and you're virtually certain to get back your principal. Treasury bills are certainly one of the best places to "store" your money while you're deciding where best to invest it.

Credit risk is the degree of chance that you won't see your money again—principal, interest, or both. Credit risk is nil for Treasury securities and high for junk bonds. The good thing about credit risk is that it's generally ascertainable, because agencies rate both government and corporate credit risks in the form of bond ratings. An unanticipated drop in a company's credit rating can cause the price of its debt (bonds) to fall substantially. At least you know what you're facing when you lend money to these entities. You can minimize your credit risk by investing in high-quality-rated assets (ratings of A and above), though you do so only by eliminating the higher-yielding investments.

Inflation risk (also called purchasing power risk) is the possibility that the returns on your investment may not keep pace with inflation. In other words, your asset might increase in price without gaining in value because of the erosive effects of inflation. Experience throughout this century in the United States supports using about 3% as a long-term inflation rate when projecting how the real value of your portfolio will grow. In other words, unless your investment grows at least 3% a year, your portfolio will actually be losing value! Based on historical returns, it's probably safe to expect the following annualized returns after inflation over long periods of time (these are called "real" returns, because they represent real increases in value).

The obvious approach to limiting your inflation risk is to invest in those assets whose expected real returns exceed zero—that is, they at least keep up with the inflation rate.

Asset	Expected Real Return
Treasury bills	0-1%
High quality bonds	2%
Foreign and high-yield bonds	3-4%
Large company stocks	7%
Small company stocks	9%
International bonds	3-4%
International stocks	7-9%
Precious metals	0-1%

Interest rate risk and reinvestment risk relate to bond investments in similar ways. Interest rate risk represents the chance that interest rates will go up or down during the course of your investment in a particular interest-bearing asset (bonds of all sorts). Financial markets will always force the price (the principal value) of a bond in a direction that matches its interest payment (coupon) to current interest rates. In short, rising interest rates will push down the price of your bond, while falling interest rates will increase the price of your bond.

Reinvestment rate risk measures the possibility that the next bond you purchase won't carry the same interest rate as the one you are cashing in. Because of reinvestment risk, you can't count on the same income stream from bond to bond, because there is no assurance that interest rates won't change. You can't even count on the same interest rate being earned on the interest you receive from the bond you have.

Both interest rate risk and reinvestment risk can be addressed by investing in a bond fund that, in turn, invests in bonds of different interest rates and maturities. In this way, you increase your chances of receiving a reasonably predictable flow of income.

The final risk I'll mention is market risk. Market risk is

the chance that the overall market may move due to some new economic information—unexpected inflation figures, an unanticipated change in interest rates, and so on. Even though the assets in your 401(k) account will probably be mutual funds (or, possibly, stock in the company that employs you), you cannot avoid this risk. It is essentially built into the market.

Harry Markowitz and His Efficient Frontier

By now, you know just about everything you need to know about the asset classes, what their risks and returns are, and how to minimize those risks. You understand dollar cost averaging and why it works, and you've heard a lot about diversification—the practice of spreading your investment dollars among several different assets to avoid being hurt by big changes in a single asset class.

Before we examine the reasons behind asset allocation—and why it's important—you ought to understand one more concept: correlation. (I promise, this is the last big statistical term I'll force on you.) Correlation is simply a mathematical relationship between the way two things change. Let me apply the term to some of the assets we've discussed to make some sense of it.

♦ Two stocks whose returns move in the same direction—one stock increases, the other stock increases—are said to be positively correlated. If their returns always move in the same direction at the same time (regardless of how much they move), the stocks are said to be *perfectly* positively correlated. In numerical terms, the correlation of positively correlated assets would range from 0 (no correlation at all) to 1.0 (perfectly positively correlated).

♦ A stock and a bond whose returns move in opposite directions—the stock return rises, the bond return falls—are said to be negatively correlated. If their returns always move in opposite directions at the same

time, the stocks are said to be *perfectly* negatively correlated. Numerically, negative correlations range from
0 (no correlation) to −1.0 (perfectly negatively correlated).

Here's how correlation can affect your investment
portfolio's performance. Let's look at two extremely rare
situations. First, suppose you have two stock funds in your
portfolio and suppose the two stock funds provide returns
that are perfectly positively correlated. What will happen is
this: when the returns on both stock funds are positive,
the return on the entire portfolio of two stock funds will
rise an amount equal to their sum. And when the returns
are negative, the portfolio's losses will be the combined loss.
In other words, perfect positive correlation results in much
wider swings in your portfolio's returns. For this reason
alone, you need to be aware that most U. S. stocks have
positively correlated returns (though perfect positive correlation is quite rare).

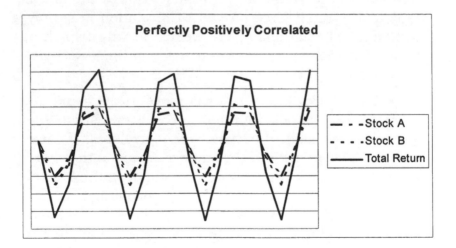

Next, suppose you have one stock fund and one bond
fund in your portfolio and suppose their returns are perfectly negatively correlated. When the stock fund provides
positive returns, the bond fund provides losses, and vice
versa. Your portfolio's total return will fall in between the

two extremes. Perfectly negative correlation greatly reduces the variability—that is, the risk—in your portfolio's returns. An ideal portfolio would be constructed with negatively correlated assets so chosen to provide the greatest return with the lowest possible risk.

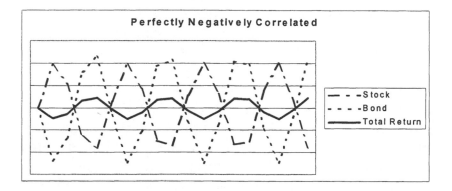

In reality, of course, perfectly correlated returns are hard to come by. Instead, you can build a portfolio consisting of imperfectly correlated assets to achieve good returns at a risk lower than either asset alone would afford. In the graph below, for example, the total return of the portfolio remains significant, yet it never reaches the extremes of either asset alone.

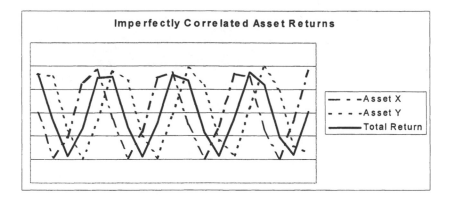

This is where Nobel Prize Winner Harry Markowitz and his Modern Portfolio Theory enter the picture. Markowitz demonstrated that you can (should!) add risky assets to a portfolio and actually reduce the risk in the total portfolio. You can do this because assets tend to move in different directions during their market cycles—in other words, rather than being perfectly positively correlated, different assets tend to be negatively or at least imperfectly correlated.

To demonstrate this to yourself, review the Perfectly Negatively Correlated graph on the previous page. By adding one risky asset (the widely varying stock fund) to another risky asset (the highly volatile bond fund), the portfolio's risk was reduced significantly. The principle is also reflected in the Imperfectly Correlated Asset Returns graph. Although risky Asset X has returns that poorly correlate with risky Asset Y, the combined portfolio still has an overall risk slightly less than either asset alone.

In his Modern Portfolio Theory, Markowitz said that it's possible to identify from a universe of risky investments a range of optimal portfolios for each level of market risk and each expected return, based on the correlations among the various available assets. Nowadays, because of the broad range of assets available, such combinations are evaluated by computer.

An example is pictured below. As you can see, the expected returns from the investments are graphed against

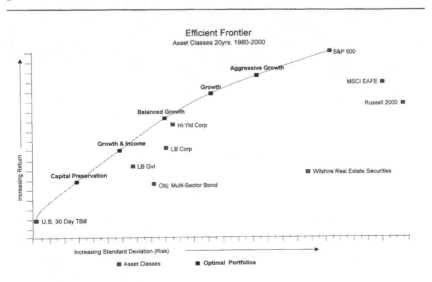

Efficient Frontier
Asset Classes 20yrs. 1980-2000

the risks presented by those investments. The portfolios which lie on the curve—the efficient portfolios—provide the highest expected return achievable for that level of risk. Portfolios below the efficient frontier, on the other hand, can achieve the same returns only by undertaking higher levels of risk. Similarly, inefficient portfolios can be constructed with the same level of risk, but their returns will be lower.

Because of the risk-reduction benefits afforded by combining numerous assets that have imperfectly or negatively correlated returns, the portfolios that comprise the efficient frontier are typically those which are most highly diversified. Less well-diversified portfolios tend to gravitate toward the center of the achievable region.

Profiting From The Scarborough Plan

The Scarborough Plan aims to maximize the power of your 401(k) plan by locating your portfolio as close to the efficient frontier as possible. The best way to do this is to include high quality mutual funds focused on all the sorts of assets that belong in your portfolio. In effect, you need diversification both within an asset class—to avoid the adverse impact of one or two badly performing assets—and diversification between asset classes—to avoid the risk associated with being in only one type of investment.

In Chapter 5, I'll discuss in some detail the components you need to look for in your company's 401(k) plan. You can't achieve good returns without good investments, so your 401(k) plan ought to offer mutual funds that have strong historical performances. And you can't get your portfolio close to the efficient frontier without being able to diversify among asset classes, so your 401(k) plan should provide choices that include stock, bond, and international mutual funds.

We've spent this whole chapter discussing the importance of investing early and regularly in a variety of asset classes. You've seen how the different assets have performed historically, both in terms of their returns and in terms of their risk or volatility. You've learned something about the different sorts of risks and how you can manage them. And you've gotten a taste of Markowitz's Modern Portfolio Theory and how proper diversification of assets can put your portfolio close to the efficient frontier, where it can achieve the highest return possible for any particular level of risk. That's what asset allocation is all about!

In the next section of this book, we'll detail how The Scarborough Plan can enable you to get your portfolio near the efficient frontier and keep it there. We'll start with an introductory chapter on 401(k) plans, so you can understand what I think a 401(k) is—and what I think it isn't.

The Scarborough Plan

1. Define in detail your retirement lifestyle.
2. Calculate exactly how much you'll need in your retirement account.
3. Determine how long it will be before you must tap into your retirement assets.
4. Start saving the required amounts now.
5. Determine your estimated Social Security income.
6. After your 401(k), rank your other investments according to the tax advantages they offer.
7. Invest your retirement savings in tax-deferred alternatives first.
8. **Start investing now. The sooner you begin, the more you earn.**
9. **Invest regularly to gain the benefits of dollar cost averaging.**
10. **Diversify your assets appropriately to maximize your returns for a given level of risk.**

SECTION II
MAXIMIZING THE POWER
OF YOUR 401(k)

4

WHAT YOUR 401(k) PLAN IS—
AND WHAT IT IS NOT

Over the past two decades, the 401(k) plan has become the most popular method employers offer their employees to establish a retirement nest egg. The first 401(k) plan was set up by the Johnson Companies as a payroll-deduction retirement savings plan on January 1, 1981. Ten months later, the Internal Revenue Service decided that the plan fit within their rules as revised by Congress in the Employee Retirement Income Security Act of 1974.

In this chapter, we're concerned about your perspective as the employee, as the participant in your company's 401(k) plan. First, we'll highlight the main rules surrounding 401(k) plans. Next, we'll review the purposes of your 401(k) plan, many of which we've considered in earlier chapters. Finally, we'll take a look at what your 401(k) shouldn't be used for, along with some of the common pitfalls that snag the uninitiated 401(k)-plan participant.

The Highlights of 401(k) Plans

Virtually any business can adopt a 401(k) plan—sole proprietorships, partnerships, limited liability corporations, and corporations. Since 1997, thanks to the Small Business Job Protection Act of 1996, even tax-exempt employers have been able to offer them. Unfortunately, state and

local governments or their agencies have not been allowed
to adopt 401(k) plans.

As of 1998, more than four-fifths of companies with at
least 1,000 employees offer 401(k) plans, and more than
three-quarters of their employees participate in the plans.

Employers may choose to match their employees' contributions to the plans to whatever extent they choose (including none), and matching contributions significantly
enhance participation rates. According to recent surveys,
participation rates range from about 60% at companies with
no match to more than 80% at companies with a match.

The company determines who is eligible to participate
in its 401(k) plan, within certain guidelines. For example,
employers can exclude the following classes of individuals
from their plans: employees with less than one year of service, employees who are under 21 years old, union mem-
bers, non-U.S. citizens, and certain part-time workers.

Contributions to the 401(k) plan can come from the
employee—through payroll deductions—or from the employer or both. The average percentage contribution cannot exceed 15% of the payroll for all eligible employees for
the entire 401(k), but the maximum individual contribution can legally reach 25%. Many companies limit individual
contributions to 15% or 20% to ensure that they don't exceed the 15% total limit. For 2000, the maximum dollar
contribution an employee can make on a pre-tax basis to a
401(k) plan is $10,500. Some companies, as I mentioned
earlier, also allow their plan participants to make contributions on an after-tax basis, thereby enabling employees
to contribute more than the $10,500 pre-tax limit.

Employers also face contribution limits that are determined both by dollar amount and by participation of so-
called highly compensated individuals. Currently, the maximum total amount that can be contributed to your 401(k)
plan each year (your contribution plus your employer's
contribution) is 25% of your pre-tax compensation or
$30,000, whichever is less. Disproportionate participation

in the plan by the company's owners or highest paid employees can reduce these annual limits.

Up to the limits established, if all contributions to your 401(k) plan are made pre-tax, they don't appear as ordinary income. Furthermore, all interest, dividends, and capital gains realized by your 401(k) account are protected from taxation until such time as you begin withdrawing funds from the account. As we discussed in earlier chapters, this feature provides outstanding growth potential compared to any other account that does not offer tax protection.

Although employers can establish vesting schedules for the contributions they make to the 401(k) accounts, all contributions made by the employee are fully vested immediately upon being made. Rollover contributions from a former employer's 401(k) plan to the new employer's 401(k) plan must also be 100% vested. Regulations require that employers adopt a vesting schedule, giving participants the right to the company's contributions should they leave the company, that progresses at least as rapidly as one of these two schedules:

Progressive or Graded Vesting Schedule	
Years of Service	Percent Vested
less than 3	0%
3	20%
4	40%
5	60%
6	80%
7 or more	100%

Breakpoint or Cliff Vesting Schedule	
Years of Service	Percent Vested
less than 5	0%
5 or more	100%

Employees also become 100% vested upon their attainment of normal retirement age, on complete or partial termination of the plan, or upon complete discontinuance of the plan. Most plans also provide for 100% vesting upon the death or disability of the employee, though they aren't required to do so.

Almost always, companies hire outside administrators to oversee their 401(k) plans. Nevertheless, it's important for you to remember that your employer can significantly influence the choices offered by your plan through the choice and oversight of the administrator. If you identify shortcomings in your 401(k) plan, ask your employer to seek changes in the plan's offerings or administration by contacting the plan administrator.

One of the critical features of any 401(k) plan is the range of investment choices offered. Although the rules governing 401(k) plans require a broad range of investment alternatives, this has been interpreted to mean a minimum of three investment alternatives offering both diversification and materially different risk-return profiles. Typically, this requirement results in at least the offering of a money market fund, a bond fund, and a stock (or equity) fund. If you read the last chapter, you'll realize that three funds won't give you the diversification you really need to get your portfolio onto the efficient frontier—that is, to realize the best gains for the risk incurred. Companies recognize this, and the actual number of investment choices offered has gradually risen to an average of eight to ten options.

401(k) plans can offer the option of borrowing against the plan account, though I'll argue later that you would typically do this only as a last resort. Any loans against the account must bear an interest rate consistent with that charged by commercial lenders for loans made under similar circumstances. The loan repayment has to be substantially level (the payments must not include a balloon payment), and the balance must be fully paid within five years unless the proceeds were used to purchase the employee's principal residence. If any of the loan provisions are not met, the entire loan gets treated as a distribution—in other words, you'll be taxed at your ordinary income tax rate on the loan, as well as pay a 10% penalty tax if you took the loan before age 59½. The real cost of the loan, though, is what we call opportunity cost—that's the growth in value that you don't get because the money you borrowed is no longer invested in a properly allocated portfolio.

Funds may also be withdrawn from your 401(k) account under certain hardship conditions—for instance, to pay medical care expenses incurred by you or your dependents. Remember, though, if you've planned adequately, you should have money set aside elsewhere to deal with these contingencies. Even if your plan offers withdrawal provisions, try to forget they exist.

These constitute the basic features available from most 401(k) plans. Now let's explore how you should—and shouldn't—use your 401(k) plan.

How You Should Use Your 401(k) Plan

All right, I'll admit it. This is so obvious it shouldn't even be necessary, but here goes, anyway. Use your 401(k) plan to prepare for your financial needs after you stop working. Any other use of your 401(k) account assets is inappropriate.

You'll get the most out of your 401(k) plan if you start early, invest a consistent amount on a regular schedule, and allocate your assets wisely. Starting early—as soon as you're eligible—ensures you the maximum number of periods during which your earnings will be compounded. Not only will the money you put into your account grow, but also the dividends, interest, and capital gains will add value to your retirement package. The more time your account has to work for you, the greater value it will attain. If you haven't signed up yet, close the book and go enroll in your company's 401(k) plan now. Take this book with you for reference.

Investing a consistent amount on a regular schedule provides you the benefits of dollar cost averaging and takes the emotions out of the investing decision. Payroll deduction accomplishes all this for you. You should already have figured out how much you can spare from each paycheck. Have that amount taken out before you even see it and you'll be amazed at how easy it is to participate fully in your 401(k) plan. In fact, for your own future self-interest, you should stretch as far as you can towards maximizing your regular contributions. As I said, if you never see it, you're unlikely to waste it. And it's always preferable to have more than you need—instead of less than you need— when retirement rolls around.

Be sure you understand the concepts I presented in Chapter 3 (and learn more about their practical application in Chapter 5), so you can choose wisely from the investment options provided by your company's 401(k) plan. Specifically, you'll want to spread your investment dollars over a range of asset classes (large company stocks; small company stocks; bonds; international stocks and bonds), and you'll want to do it in a way that maximizes your return for the level of risk you're willing to assume (get your portfolio as close as possible to the efficient frontier).

Remember that you're using the 401(k) to save for your retirement because the plan enables you to protect your investment from taxes right up until you need the money. It is there to maximize the amount of money working for you. This is all the more reason to fight any temptation to use this tax-protected money for anything but retirement unless some terrible hardship exhausts all your other resources.

Remember, too, that your 401(k) plan may be the last leg your retirement stool has to stand on. Social Security benefits will almost certainly begin well after you encounter retirement living expenses, and even then, the benefits are likely to be far less than you'd like them to be. If you expect this one-legged stool to support you, then the one leg will have to be pretty substantial.

Your retirement strategy—assuming, as it does, that you will live forever—depends upon having a substantial amount of principal in place to generate the cash flow necessary to meet the expenses you're likely to encounter throughout a long, comfortable retirement. Think of every dollar you put into your 401(k) account as a permanent investment. Plan on never seeing it again. You're going to live forever off its proceeds, not the principal.

How You Should Not Use Your 401(k) Plan

A couple came to see me just last week with their great idea.

"We need $30,000 to build a new garage, so we thought we'd borrow the money from Dan's 401(k) account," Sharon said.

"You planning to retire in that garage?" I asked. "That doesn't sound like retirement planning to me."

"What's the big deal?" Dan asked. "I'm paying myself interest on the loan."

"Right," I said, "you're paying yourself, what, 8% interest? And the market's moving up at, what, 12% a year? So basically, you're throwing away $100 a month in retirement cash for your new garage."

Think back to the beginning of this chapter and you'll certainly come up with a few ways you could use your 401(k) plan—and absolutely shouldn't. I'll mention three.

You could use your 401(k) account as a savings account, a source of ready cash. Well, you could, except you can't. Yes, there is (at least) one way that all the assets in your 401(k) account could be converted to cash and presented to you in the form of a check. Just quit your job and close your account. There are only about three problems with this idea. The first problem is the not-so-little matter of withholding tax. If you have your now-former employer write you that check, you'll discover that the check is 20% smaller than you might have expected. Why? Unless you roll your 401(k) assets directly into an IRA rollover account, your employer (or fund administrator) must withhold 20% of the total amount of cash from your distribution. Even hardship withdrawals are subject to the 20% withholding.

The second problem has to do with taxation and penalties. If you fail to reinvest your distribution into another qualified retirement account, you must pay both ordinary income tax on the distribution (the withholding may cover this) and a 10 % penalty tax if you receive funds before you reach age 59½. So far, then, you've received only 70% of what you had in your "savings" account. On top of that, you've probably under-withheld: you'll have to come up with additional federal tax plus your state income tax as well!

The final problem relates to what we agreed is the purpose of your 401(k) account. You're spending money that was already earmarked for your retirement. By eroding this account, you may miss your investment targets and have to retire later or downgrade your retirement lifestyle. Neither option is desirable.

You could also use your 401(k) as a source of loans. That's not usually a good idea. First, you'll have to pay about the same interest as you'd face with a commercial loan—interest that you can't deduct from your income tax anyway. The loan term will probably be less favorable than what the bank would give you—the limit for full repayment is five years. Your bank will give you more than that to buy a car or boat or finance your child's education.

Besides it being a bad loan source, it's a bad deal for your retirement. When you borrow funds from your 401(k) account, you keep those funds from growing. You may think you're earning interest, but you're actually missing the chance to let your assets earn dividends, interest, and capital gains for you, amounting to a serious long-term earnings loss. Besides all that, you repay your loan with after-tax dollars, and those dollars get taxed again when you start taking distributions during your retirement years. The only winner is Uncle Sam.

And one final caveat: if you decide to leave your current employment during the course of your loan repayment, the loan is usually fully callable—that means the employer can demand the immediate repayment of the balance of the loan. If you need to borrow money, go to the bank. Get a home-equity loan or line of credit. Don't mortgage your retirement funds.

How about using your 401(k) funds to buy a home? That's allowed, right? Yes, it's allowed, but it may not be in your best interest. For all the reasons I've already mentioned. Plus another one: the maximum loan you'll be able to take is $50,000 (assuming your account amounts to at least $100,000 and you have no other loans outstanding). As I said before, go to the bank. Mortgage your house, not your retirement.

Here are some other ways you could (*but should not*) misuse your 401(k) plan:

- ◆ "Accidentally" make your contributions post-tax
- ◆ Take inappropriate loans
- ◆ Make withdrawals out of fear for what might happen in the economy
- ◆ Use market timing as an "investment" strategy
- ◆ Engage in "day trading"
- ◆ Put all your money into company stock
- ◆ Allocate your assets poorly (or not at all)
- ◆ Ignore your account statements
- ◆ Follow investment tips from "experts," such as your butcher or dry cleaner
- ◆ Fail to change your allocations as conditions change
- ◆ Fail to adjust your contributions as your income rises
- ◆ Fail to contribute enough to get your employer's full match
- ◆ Fail to participate because you "can't afford it"

This chapter has been a very general introduction to 401(k) plans. In Chapter 5, I'll lead you through exactly what to look for in your own 401(k) plan. We'll discuss asset allocation in more detail and consider some of the services and features found in a good 401(k) plan. And I'll outline your options if your 401(k) doesn't measure up.

The Scarborough Plan

1. Define in detail your retirement lifestyle.
2. Calculate exactly how much you'll need in your retirement account.
3. Determine how long it will be before you must tap into your retirement assets.
4. Start saving the required amounts now.
5. Determine your estimated Social Security income.
6. After your 401(k), rank your other investments according to the tax advantages they offer.
7. Invest your retirement savings in tax-deferred alternatives first.
8. Start investing now. The sooner you begin, the more you earn.
9. Invest regularly to gain the benefits of dollar cost averaging.
10. Diversify your assets appropriately to maximize your returns for a given level of risk.
11. **Maximize the contributions—yours and your employer's—to your 401(k) plan.**
12. **Minimize the withdrawals from your 401(k) account.**

5

WHAT YOUR 401(k) PLAN SHOULD BE

One of my retirement advisors told me this story. A company top executive came in with his 401(k) statement, because he was concerned about how best to allocate his contributions.

"My plan has thirty choices of assets," Jeffrey told her. "I had no time to evaluate each one, so I just put 5% of my contribution in twenty funds that I selected randomly."

My advisor did exactly the right thing.

"Jeffrey," she said, "let's take a look at your plan and see how we can make it work best for you."

Most of the time, you won't be blessed with so many alternatives you'll have trouble picking out the best ones. On the other hand, an increasing number of plans include direct brokerage links that enable the participant to tap into the entire universe of investment options. In this situation, I encourage clients to allocate their assets among a variety of mutual funds to avoid the perils of investing in individual stocks and bonds. Your 401(k) plan will likely fall somewhere in between these two extremes.

What you need to know, then, is how to figure out whether your 401(k) stands somewhere in this acceptable middle ground or not. In other words, how many choices and which features constitute the minimal plan? And what can you do if your plan crosses the line separating the *okay* from the *oh, no*? That's what this chapter is all about.

Best-Case and Worst-Case Scenarios

Before you can decide whether your 401(k) plan fits the best-case scenario or the worst-case scenario or—more than likely—the in-between-case scenario, you need some criteria by which to judge it. For convenience, I'll divide the criteria into three groups: assets, features, and services.

By assets I mean the investment choices offered by your 401(k) plan. You remember from Chapter 3 that asset allocation represents the most important determinant of your retirement account's growth and earning potential. How you allocate your investment dollars will dictate how those dollars work for you over the next five or ten or twenty years. It should be pretty obvious that good allocation requires a variety of good assets to allocate *to*, so what you're looking for here are both good quality and an adequate quantity from which to choose.

As you'll see, the best-case scenario provides a broad range of asset classes. In the worst-case scenario, your 401(k) plan would offer you the bare minimum required by the rules: one money market account, one bond fund, and one stock—your company's. With any luck, your 401(k) lies closer to the best-case than to the worse-case scenario.

Features include those options allowed but not required by the regulations governing 401(k) plans. Among features you might find a matching contribution from your company, unlimited transfers of funds among your investment options (assets), liberal loan provisions, and others that we'll consider later in this chapter. Features are simply those elements that can change your 401(k) from plain vanilla into the banana split of 401(k) plans.

With features, it's abundance that creates the best-case scenario, even if you don't take advantage of them all. Fewer features, on the other hand, make for a less desirable 401(k) plan. Features can be expensive for your company, though, so you're likely to encounter greater resistance in increasing the features than you might confront in broadening the asset selections. Added features could also cost you more, though, because those expenses can often be charged against the plan's assets. So be careful what you ask for.

What do I mean by services? At some restaurants, the pinnacle of services is a drive-through window. At other restaurants, the maitre d'hôtel escorts you and your friend to a quiet, candlelit table in the corner, eases your chair under you, and drapes your linen napkin onto your lap. Some 401(k) plans let you know every once in a while what's up with your account; others provide secure, unlimited Internet access to your account with real-time valuation. You get the idea.

The worst-case 401(k) plan is a fast-food restaurant staffed by acrimonious high school dropouts. The best-case 401(k) plan is a five-star gourmet restaurant with an extensive wine list and someone whose job it is to explain it. How much your company is willing to pay determines where you go out for dinner.

Let's take a closer look at assets, features, and services.

What You Need for Effective Asset Allocation

Before we look at specific assets, let's briefly review three critical concepts: diversification, correlation, and the efficient frontier. If you skipped Chapter 3, this might be a good time to go back and read it. Understanding these ideas really helps to appreciate the importance of assets and their proper allocation.

Diversification is investment shorthand for *don't put all your eggs in one basket.* Investing all your money in one stock is like betting on one horse to win in a field of twelve. If your horse wins, that's great. If your horse places second or third or last, you lose everything. If, on the other hand, you bet two dollars on the six favorite horses to show, you stand a decent chance of a couple winning tickets. You may make less, but you've risked less—and it's much less likely that you'll lose everything.

Investments resemble horse races in that way. No one can pick winners all the time. And diversification represents the best way of hedging your bets in such an uncertain environment. Spreading your investment dollars among asset classes—stocks, bonds, cash—minimizes the risks presented by the ups and downs of each individual market. Within the asset classes, allocating your investment dollars among several individual investments (a multitude of stocks, say, or a handful of mutual funds) greatly reduces the impact of one bad choice on your portfolio's performance. Diversification, in short, is your best strategy for reducing risk.

How much diversification is enough diversification? Financial experts will tell you that you reach the limits of risk reduction through diversification once you have between twenty and thirty stocks (or bonds or whatever asset) in your portfolio. After that, you still get diversification, but the diversification does not further reduce your overall risk. Mutual funds, as I mentioned before, can give you instant diversification within a particular asset class, because mutual funds typically consist of between 100 and 150 different stocks or bonds.

Correlation measures how different assets perform in relation to each other. You can use information about correlation to get more bang for your diversification buck. Why? Because the less each investment tracks the other investments, the more risk reduction benefit you get from adding it to your portfolio. Ideally, you want investments that have negative correlations with other investments in your portfolio. In reality, though, you'll probably have to settle for low positive correlations.

Investing internationally, by the way, gives you the best of both diversification and correlation. Many foreign markets have very low correlations with the performance of U.S. markets. By choosing an appropriately broad mix of investments in several other markets, you gain added protection against declining markets here in the U.S.

We investigated the notion of efficient frontiers in some detail back in Chapter 3. The efficient frontier represents those investments (portfolios) that produce the greatest returns for a given level of risk or, alternatively, risk the least for a given rate of return. Your objective—or the objective of your retirement advisor—is to design a retirement portfolio that lies on this efficient frontier (or as close to it as possible). And that portfolio will be unique to you, because every investor has a different risk tolerance. While you'd love to shoot for the highest returns attainable, you may not like the risks that go along with them. Remember: you have to be able to live with the ups and downs your portfolio will experience, and the greater the risk, the wider those swings are likely to be.

In summary, what you'd like your 401(k) plan to offer you is a wide range of investment alternatives so you can gain the benefits of diversification. You'd like the available instruments to have returns that are poorly correlated to help reduce your risk even further. And you'd like to be able to allocate these choices in a way that your overall portfolio lies close to the efficient frontier—that is, gives you the best possible rate of return for the level of risk you're willing to assume.

Asset Allocation and Your 401(k) Plan

Okay, so that's the theory behind maximizing the returns of your 401(k). What, specifically, do you look for in your 401(k) plan to determine whether your goals are attainable?

First, you want to be certain that your 401(k) plan offers at least what the law requires. While the odds are extremely slim that it doesn't meet the requirements, it's important to know what the plan must have, just so you can be sure. Here's what the law says are the bare minimum requirements for asset classes offered by a 401(k) plan: you must be allowed to choose from at least three investment alternatives that satisfy four criteria.

One, each individual investment alternative must be diversified. Mutual funds containing stocks from several industries or bonds from several companies or government entities would probably satisfy this requirement.

Two, the alternatives must offer significantly different risk and return characteristics. Three different mutual funds consisting of growth stocks would fail this requirement, but one stock fund, one bond fund, and one money market fund would probably qualify.

Three, the choices should enable you to design a portfolio with risk and return characteristics within reasonable ranges.

Finally, an appropriate combination of the choices should minimize your overall risk for a given return. In other words, the (minimum) three choices should be mixable in a way that gets your portfolio onto an efficient frontier for those alternatives.

Beyond the minimum, though, you'd like a 401(k) plan that provides selections within at least these asset classes:

- Growth stock mutual funds (large-, mid-, and small-cap stocks)
- Value stock mutual funds (large-, mid-, and small-cap stocks)
- International stock mutual funds
- International bond mutual funds
- Corporate bond mutual funds
- Government bond mutual funds
- Guaranteed investment contracts (GICs)
- Market index funds
- Your company's stock (optional)

In Chapter 3, we discussed most of these asset types and listed their historical returns and risks (as measured by the variability of their returns). As you recall, the best returns for their risk come from growth stocks. Stock mutual funds often differ according to the size of the companies that constitute them. "Cap" refers to market capitalization, the overall dollar value of the shares of stock outstanding in the market. To determine market capitalization, simply multiply the number of shares outstanding by the current market price per share. Market caps over $8 billion represent large-caps, while values below $1 billion or so get classified as small-caps. Market capitalizations in-between earn mid-cap status. Though the risks and returns of the different size companies will vary, owning one of each stock mutual fund provides you less diversification benefit than owning, say, one stock fund, one bond fund, and one international fund. Why? Because the stock mutual fund returns will tend to be highly correlated, while the returns of three altogether different types of asset funds will tend to be less correlated. Remember correlation?

Growth and income stock funds consist of stocks in companies with long histories of consistent growth and reliable dividend payments. These funds provide lower risks (less variability) at the expense of somewhat lower returns.

International stock funds invest in stocks of other countries. They may specialize in rapidly growing, but less well-established, markets—these are called emerging market funds—or they may include stocks from countries in a few neighboring countries—these are called regional funds—or they may contain stocks from both foreign countries and the U.S.—these are called global funds. Whatever their makeup, international stock funds may increase returns and reduce risk by providing returns that do not move in sync with domestic stock returns.

Corporate bond funds should contain bonds from several different companies (preferably in a variety of industries) and of several different maturities. This type of diversification provides protection against some of the risks we discussed in Chapter 3 (especially credit and reinvestment risks).

Government bond funds, for similar reasons, should include bonds of several maturities. Credit risk, presumably, is not a concern; reinvestment and inflation risks, though, have to be considered.

Guaranteed investment contracts promise the payment of a specific rate of interest on the funds invested over a specified period of time. These instruments, sold by insurance companies, offer little protection against inflation and reinvestment risks. Nevertheless, they provide diversification for your portfolio, as well as a reasonable choice under certain economic conditions.

Market index funds contain assets that mirror the makeup of a stated market index. An S&P 500 fund, for example, would include the 500 S&P stocks in proportions that reflect those found in the S&P 500 Stock Index. Other popular index funds mimic the Russell 2000 (2,000 small companies) and the Lehman Brothers Government and Corporate Bond index (investment-grade bonds).

Money market funds are as close to cash as an asset can get. These funds invest in very short-term, high-quality assets, like certificates of deposit (CDs), Treasury bills, and commercial paper. Although they are especially subject to interest rate fluctuations, they beat leaving the cash lying around earning nothing. Money market funds represent a reasonable place to keep your investment while you're deciding how best to allocate the funds. But don't let your assets linger there very long.

Finally, there's stock in the company you work for. When your company uses its own stock as part of the 401(k) plan, you might invest in it willingly or by default. First, the company may include it as an option in your participant directed 401(k) plan, so that you could choose to include it in your asset allocation. Second, the company may match some amount of your 401(k) contributions in its stock, rather than allowing you to allocate the match to other assets.

I have basically two thoughts about company stock. One, ordinarily you should limit your company's stock to no more than 10% of your portfolio. The main reason has to do with diversification of your life's assets. You're already depending upon the success of the company to provide you an income while you're working. Depending upon the company's success to provide you a substantial retirement nest egg is another form of putting all those eggs into one basket. It's just too risky. Two, if your company matches your 401(k) contribution in company stock, find out whether you can transfer out of company stock and into some other asset(s). Sure, a company match is good, but it would be much better if you could allocate that match yourself. Whether your boss believes it or not, there might be an investment better than your company's stock.

Unfortunately, most 401(k) plans will include substantially fewer investment choices than the asset classes just described, though the trend is to provide additional choices. In many cases, your company will be receptive to requests to expand the assets available for investment, especially if it does not mean increased costs to the company. Most company executives participate in company 401(k) plans, so they will be interested in having the best plan the company can afford. A few well-chosen words about diversification and asset allocation and efficient frontiers should suffice to grab their attention and gain their support for expanding the investment choices in your plan.

What You Want in 401(k) Plan Features

Besides the requirement of three assets that offer different profiles of risks and returns, the law establishes additional features that 401(k) plans may (but not must) have. You'd like your plan to have all the features allowed by law, whether or not you will actually use them. And whether or not you actually should use them. The greater the number of features described below, the greater the flexibility you will have in managing your 401(k) assets to your advantage. We will discuss some of the features that are most common and most desirable. In general, the more of these features your plan offers, the better the plan.

Don't borrow from your 401(k) plan. It keeps the borrowed portion of your assets from growing. The real cost of borrowing is not the interest you pay, but the cost of lost opportunities.

Loan provisions. The rules allow you to take loans from your 401(k) plan, but they do not require your plan to have such provisions. Before mentioning the restrictions to such provisions, here's the most important rule to bear in mind: don't borrow from your 401(k) plan. Okay, so that isn't one of the government's rules, it's one of mine. But, as we have already discussed, borrowing from your 401(k) hurts. It keeps the borrowed portion of your assets from growing. The real cost of borrowing is not the interest you pay, but the cost of lost opportunities. Plus, you end up paying back the loan with after-tax income that will be taxed yet again years from now when you start taking money out of your 401(k) plan. Never fall into the trap of viewing your 401(k) plan as a potential source of easy cash—I guarantee you'll regret it later.

The allowable loan features are mighty restrictive, anyway. Unless the loan meets the three criteria listed below, it will be treated as a distribution and, thus, face not only taxation, but also an early withdrawal penalty of 10% of the value of the loan. To avoid the taxes and penalty, the loan:

- Must be repaid in full within five years (unless it is used to buy your principal residence)
- Must have a payment schedule with essentially level payments (at least quarterly) spread over the duration of the loan
- Must satisfy these maximum dollar limits (whichever is less)
  - $50,000 less any existing loans, or
  - The greater of $10,000 or 50% of the vested account balance

Accordingly, here are the important break points along with their maximum loan amounts:

If your vested account balance is:	You may borrow up to:
$10,000 or less	full vested balance
$10,001 to $20,000	$10,000
$20,001 to $100,000	50% of vested account
over $100,000	$50,000

In addition to these limits, your company can set limits below which your vested account balance may not fall, so you may face additional restrictions.

One final bit of good news and one of bad news about 401(k) plan loan provisions. The good news is that there are no restrictions as to how you use the proceeds of your loan. The bad news could come if you decide to change employment while you still owe on the loan. The company could choose to call the full amount of the loan at the time you (or they, for that matter) terminate your employment. They could also allow you to transfer the loan to another qualified 401(k) plan. Another reason to be nice to the company when you quit (and to be sure beforehand that the new company will allow you to transfer your loan into their 401(k) plan).

Matching contributions. Look for your company to provide some type of match to the contributions you make (or even to make contributions that do not depend upon your contribution amount). Nowadays, about 5 out of 6 companies do. A typical employer matching contribution rate equals 50% of the first 6% you contribute to your 401(k) plan, for a maximum of 3% of your income. About one-third of employers that provide a matching contribution follow some variation on this theme. Obviously, matching every dollar of your contribution with a 50 cent addition will greatly enhance the value of your 401(k) plan by giving you an immediate 50% return on your investment (if you invest the 6%). This, by itself, should make you run to your plan administrator and sign up immediately. And participate at least to the extent that your employer provides a match.

Despite the goodwill generated by matching your contributions, your company knows better than to give you access to that match without proving your loyalty to the firm. Seven out of ten companies require some wait before allowing you full access to the matching portion of your 401(k) plan (and its earnings).

Here, again, the law protects you to an extent. Your company cannot hang onto "their" portion of "your" 401(k) plan indefinitely. In fact, they have two choices (mentioned earlier) as to how they allow you to gain access to, or vest into, their matching funds. Unfortunately, you have no say in the matter of vesting. It depends exclusively upon decisions made when the plan was established or revised.

Perhaps the most commonly employed vesting schedule starts at one year of service and adds 20% annually, so that you become fully vested after your fifth year of employment by the company. Few force you to stay seven years to get your matching contribution, and fewer still employ a schedule that follows the second alternative.

Besides the amount of your company's matching contribution, you should be interested in how you'll be allowed to allocate it. In the worst case, your company will match your contribution in company stock and allow you no control in the matching contribution.

In the best case, allocation of the matching contributions will be completely under your control, just as your own contributions are. If the company matches your contribution by putting company stock into your plan, find out whether you can cash that stock in and reallocate the funds according to the allocation plan you have established. Otherwise, your company's match may turn out to be far less valuable (and far riskier) than you'd like. Ideally, then, you want to be able to allocate your employer's matching contribution exactly the same way you allocate your own contribution.

Withdrawals

Withdrawals will be taxed as ordinary income and, if you are under 59½ when you take out funds, you will face the 10% early withdrawal tax penalty. There are, though, a few exceptions to the tax penalty:

- If you face extraordinary medical expenses (more than 7.5% of your income) or if you become severely disabled.
- If you get divorced and must split your 401(k) assets, your ex (but not you) gets to withdraw his or her share.
- If you die, your beneficiaries get your proceeds.
- If you are fifty-five or older and leave your job.
- If you roll the money to an IRA Rollover account.

With the possible exception of the last two avoidance methods, it's hard to imagine hoping for any of these events to transpire just to save a 10% tax penalty.

There is one other way to make withdrawals without suffering the tax penalty. You can take your money in equal distributions based upon your life expectancy. For this, you'll need to check out the Internal Revenue Service tables to determine how much longer you have to live and, thus, what level of withdrawal you're allowed to make. Unless you're already well into your fifties or have amassed a huge 401(k) account, the size of these regular checks is bound to be pretty small.

All that being said, you'd still like to be able to make withdrawals if the need should arrive. Check with your plan administrator to see whether your plan allows them. If it doesn't, ask whether it might be changed to enable participants to take withdrawals according to what the law allows.

After-tax contributions. About one-third of all 401(k) plans allow participants to make contributions from after-tax earnings. Making such contributions benefits you in several specific situations, but be certain—before you invest dollars that have already been taxed—that the investment is definitely earmarked for your retirement. Because of tax penalties you can face upon withdrawal of these contributions, other investments make more sense if you are making them for purposes other than retirement.

When you are certain the after-tax contributions will be used for retirement, be certain (first!) that you already contribute pre-tax dollars to the allowable limits. Furthermore, the closer you are to retirement and the smaller your account value in relation to what you've calculated it needs to be, the more likely you will want (or need) to invest after-tax dollars in order to reach your retirement goals.

So it's worth asking whether your company plan allows after-tax contributions to provide you even greater flexibility in managing your retirement assets. One caveat: after-tax contributions are not eligible for rollover into an IRA, so you'll have to take a distribution of your after-tax contributions if you ever need to move your 401(k) plan.

Immediate eligibility. Companies can establish service requirements before offering participation in their 401(k) plans. They can limit participation to employees 21 years or older (but they cannot set an upper age limit), and they can require up to one year of service before allowing employees to make elective contributions to the plan. Obviously, either of these limitations delays your initial investment and you lose that opportunity to earn returns. If you're looking at moving to another company, check their policy. The best 401(k) plans allow you to make elective contributions (and begin to make matching contributions) as soon as you begin employment with the company. Especially with the number of job changes the average individual is likely to make during a career, you don't want to give up a year of pre-tax, tax-deferred investment every time you change companies. Look for immediate eligibility in your 401(k) plan.

Investment advice. The regulations draw a line between investment education and investment advice. Your company can, for example, provide you with model portfolios and suggested asset allocations to achieve your retirement goals. Commercially available software can help you estimate your future retirement income needs and determine your investment time horizons. And it can aid you in determining your own personal risk tolerance and how it fits into various asset allocation schemes.

Don't expect your company to provide much in the way of advice. But this is changing. Although employers are protected, to an extent, from bearing the responsibility for investment losses of its 401(k) plan participants, most eschew even the appearance of providing investment advice. Why? Because this is America, and anybody can sue anybody for anything. Liability concerns, then, significantly limit giving of advice.

Investment style. Investment style has nothing to do

with the color tie you wear when you invest in your 401(k) plan. Rather, it has to do with the investment style of the different assets within your 401(k) plan portfolio. Most of those assets will be mutual funds, and all of those mutual funds will state their investment style—"aggressive growth stock" or "growth and income" or something like that. What matters to you is not so much the label they put on their investment style as their consistency in adhering to whatever style they actually follow. Let's use the two examples just mentioned. If you have allocated funds to both an aggressive growth stock mutual fund (high risk, high return) and a growth and income fund (lower risk, lower return) to take advantage of diversification, imperfect correlations, and the efficient frontier we've been discussing, you don't want to find out somewhere down the line that the fund managers are investing in exactly the same stocks. My main point is this: you can't judge a fund by its name. You have to take a closer look.

All mutual funds report on the individual stocks or bonds or whatever that comprise the fund, including their relative proportions. If your "aggressive growth stock" mutual fund contains nothing but large, stable companies or utility companies or automobile manufacturers, it's more like a growth and income fund. The name may be there for historical reasons or marketing purposes. Who knows? Take a look at the list of assets owned by the mutual fund before you allocate your own assets there. Be sure their assets match their stated style. And even if everything looks all right when you begin investing, keep track of its constituents, because fund managers and even fund objectives can change without their names being changed in parallel. If you don't know how a mutual fund actually behaves, you'll end up allocating your assets unwisely.

How does this apply to your own 401(k) plan management? Just this: if the funds from which you can choose remain faithful to their investment styles, your job will be easier. If they don't, you might want to start lobbying for your company to look for a different set of mutual funds for the 401(k) plan.

Record keepers and fund managers. Record keepers are the people you contact in order to make various sorts of changes to your 401(k) plan, including asset allocations, in-service withdrawals, transfers, and so on. Fund managers are the individuals who actually manage the mutual funds within the 401(k) plan. They ought to be two different sets of people. In more than a quarter of companies, though, the record keeper is also the mutual fund or investment management firm. Nearly a third use an independent benefit consulting firm, while a tiny minority do the record keeping themselves.

If your record keeper is also your fund manager, there's a natural potential for a conflict of interest. Here's why: say you call your record keeper to transfer your funds to a rollover IRA because you're leaving the company. Your record keeper might turn around (perhaps in the form of a different person or department) and try to sell you on the value of using one of their mutual fund company's rollover IRA options. Or they might encourage you to leave your 401(k) account where it is—with the old company—so they (the fund managers) don't lose income, which generally relies on the level of overall fund assets. Either way, they may not always have your interests foremost, so beware.

This may sound like a small matter, because, after all, you can always say "no." Still, it's yet another hassle you'd like to avoid. Look for your record keeper and fund manager to come from completely separate organizations. Otherwise, point out the obvious conflict of interest to your company representative.

Will your company think you're nuts for asking for all these features in your 401(k) plan? Probably not. Instead, they'll recognize your thoroughness and attention to important details. In fact, they're likely to be glad somebody is watching out for the interests of all the plan participants.

What Services to Look For in Your 401(k) Plan

The rules require the important services from your 401(k) plan, so the list of additional services that you'd like is rather shorter than the features list we just considered. Most important of the required services is valuation, which includes the reporting of your account's activities, allocations, earnings, and overall value. The problem is, the regulations require valuation at least annually, and that's a long time to find out how your account is faring. You'd like to be able to determine your account's makeup and value anytime, on a moment's notice. In fact, this should present no problem to your record keeper, as everything about your account lives on a computer somewhere. So two services you should ask for in your 401(k) plan are daily valuation and voice response units. For similar reasons of timeliness and flexibility, you want the minimum number of restrictions on your ability to change your allocation of assets.

Daily valuation. Daily valuation is exactly what it sounds like—a computerized system tracks your investment activity and updates the value of your account every business day. Most systems track your investments as units rather than as dollars, so you may have to multiply the number of units by the market price of the particular investment, but even that is unlikely. Computers can multiply faster than you can, anyway, and your record keeper will probably quote your account value in both ways (units and dollars).

Besides giving you up to the day values for your 401(k) account assets, daily valuation allows more timely investments of your contributions, transfers, and withdrawals. Distributions can often be made more quickly, because a formal account valuation does not have to be made by some person who's likely to be much less interested than you are in completing the distribution transaction. With daily valuation, the account valuation is already done, automatically, every day.

There is one subtle disadvantage of daily valuation that you need to avoid. Let's call it impulsiveness. Human nature being what it is, you might look at your valuation one day and think some of the assets are not performing as well as they ought. Your next step might be to reshuffle the assets in your account. History tells us that such changes are extremely unlikely to be wise. So learn from history before your retirement account becomes history. Checking on your account's value every day is fine; messing with the account every day is stupid. Don't be stupid.

Most plans—more than three out of four—include daily valuation. See that yours does.

Voice response units. Voice response unit is a fancy term for your 401(k) plan's voicemail. You pick up the phone (or, increasingly, go onto the Internet) and access your account information whenever you get the urge. In some cases, you'll be able to perform certain activities through the same system. The same caveats apply to voice response units as apply to daily valuation. While timely information is powerful, daily decisions based on that information can be powerfully unwise.

Unlimited allocation changes. Because conditions change, you'd like to be able to change your investment allocations whenever new circumstances warrant. How often you can actually change your allocations, though, depends upon what your plan allows. The rules on this subject can get complicated, because they depend on the volatility of the available asset choices. At the very least, the regulations say, a 401(k) plan with any mixture of funds must allow transfers among the funds at least quarterly. Plans that offer riskier (in other words, more volatile) investment alternatives must allow transfers more often.

What you would like is the unrestricted ability to move assets among the funds available in your 401(k) plan. Not only would you like the ability unrestricted, but also you'd like the transfers to be free of penalties and charges. You might not be able to realize this ideal, though, because the regulations do not forbid withdrawal penalties, fees, and other restrictions on asset transfers.

In summary, when you're looking at the services provided by your 401(k) plan, focus on such important options as daily valuation, voice response units, and unrestricted allocation changes. They provide you the information and investing flexibility you need to manage your 401(k) plan for maximum returns.

When Your 401(k) Plan Does Not Measure Up

When you meet with your company representative to size up your 401(k) plan, make sure you're prepared to ask all the right questions. The best approach is to take this checklist along with you.

Check off the features and services offered by your 401 (k) plan and ask about the ones not offered. Since no two plans are alike, you should consider the following priorities.

PRIORITY ONE
- ❏ Immediate eligibility
- ❏ Wide range of investment alternatives (15-20 or more)
- ❏ Company match (dollar for dollar is best; 50% up to 6% of gross income or better is acceptable)
- ❏ Investment advice available

PRIORITY TWO
- ❏ Vesting (immediate is best, 20% per year is acceptable)
- ❏ Employee directs investment of company match
- ❏ Maximum contribution permitted is at least 15%
- ❏ Daily valuation

PRIORITY THREE
- ❏ Loan provisions
- ❏ Unrestricted number of allocation changes
- ❏ Voice response capability

PRIORITY FOUR
- ❏ Pre- and post-tax contributions permitted
- ❏ In-service withdrawals
- ❏ Separate record-keeper / fund manager

Once you have completed the checklist, you'll be able to determine how well your 401(k) measures up. Your first indication will be the number of boxes checked—generally, the more features and services, the better your 401(k) plan will be. If there are more boxes checked than not, chances are your plan is reasonably acceptable. If only a handful of check marks appear, your plan may be seriously flawed.

But it is not simply the number of boxes checked or not checked that ultimately matters as much as *which* boxes are checked. While many features and services are desirable, others should be viewed as critical. Voice response units, for example, would be nice. A broad variety of investment choices, on the other hand, would be essential.

Now you're ready to sit down with your plan documents (or speak with your company representative) to figure out how good your 401(k) plan is and whether it's worth fighting for the elements it lacks. As I mentioned above, I'd certainly ask for as many asset types as possible and unrestricted fund transfers, but I wouldn't risk my charming reputation in an angry battle over the company's unwillingness to provide investment advice. Instead, I'd suggest you consider the options in Chapter 8 for finding good investment advice.

Which brings us to the question of what to do if your 401(k) offers fewer choices than the office soda machine.

Start by calling or meeting with your plan administrator. You may find that the missing features resulted from ignorance ("We never thought of that") instead of active decisions ("We decided we didn't need that" or "Our employees wouldn't pay for the added cost of those features").

You may have to fight just plain inertia. Your best weapon in that battle is information. Show the company how the missing features cripple the participants or discourage participation or lower morale — whatever hits the hot buttons in your company. Armed with the facts, you'll at least be able to point out—in the nicest way, of course—the value of your recommendations and ask them to deal with it.

In this chapter, we've considered all the elements of a good 401(k) plan—its requirements, its features, and its services. In Chapter 6, we'll take a tour of Individual Retirement Accounts (IRAs), not because they're part of your 401(k) plan, but because they complement your 401(k) account in a number of ways. Should you be investing in an IRA when you already have a 401(k) plan? Is a Roth IRA right for you? Unless you're sure of the answers to all these questions, you ought not to skip it.

The Scarborough Plan

1. Define in detail your retirement lifestyle.
2. Calculate exactly how much you'll need in your retirement account.
3. Determine how long it will be before you must tap into your retirement assets.
4. Start saving the required amounts now.
5. Determine your estimated Social Security income.
6. After your 401(k), rank your other investments according to the tax advantages they offer.
7. Invest your retirement savings in tax-deferred alternatives first.

8. Start investing now. The sooner you begin, the more you earn.

9. Invest regularly to gain the benefits of dollar cost averaging.

10. Diversify your assets appropriately to maximize your returns for a given level of risk.

11. Maximize the contributions—yours and your employer's—to your 401(k) plan.

12. Minimize the withdrawals from your 401(k) account.

13. **Understand the options offered by your 401(k) plan.**

14. **Seek improvements in your 401(k) plan where necessary.**

6

COMPLEMENTING YOUR 401(k) WITH IRAS

"Look, Mike," said Kyle, one of my longtime clients, "I need to save more than I'm allowed to put into my 401(k)."

Oh, if only more people were like Kyle!

"Now what do I do?" he asked.

"Kyle" I answered, "let's talk about your IRA options."

The goal of this chapter is not to make you an expert on Individual Retirement Accounts (IRAs). Instead, in keeping with our goal of maximizing the power of your 401(k), we're going to discuss three types of IRAs and how they should be used to complement your 401(k) plan and ensure yourself a successful retirement. We'll talk about some of the specific rules governing those IRAs and how to distinguish between them. And, of course, we'll consider how decisions about IRAs will influence decisions you make about your 401(k) plan. We are mainly interested in how your IRA can interact with your 401(k) to help you achieve your retirement goals, not with the nuts and bolts of how IRAs work.

Among the many IRA types that can add value to your retirement account, we will discuss only traditional IRAs, the new Roth IRAs, and rollover IRAs. If you work for a smaller company or for yourself, simple IRAs and SEP-IRAs are also beneficial (but in those cases, you probably wouldn't have a 401(k) plan and wouldn't be reading this book). And as far as Educational IRAs, that strikes me as an oxymoron. Even though they have some features in common, if you're putting away money for your child's education, that's an educational savings plan (ESP), not an individual retirement account (IRA). For those reasons, we'll focus our attention on traditional, Roth, and rollover IRAs.

Traditional IRAs

The original IRA began in 1974, but many changes have taken place since then. Originally, everybody who contributed to an IRA was entitled to a tax deduction for his or her contribution. That ended December 31, 1986, when income limits and company retirement plans phased out the deductibility for certain people. Lately, changes have benefited some of those groups, while also relieving the tax penalty for certain types of withdrawals.

Traditional IRAs allow you to contribute up to $2,000 a year that grows tax-deferred. In that sense, they provide one of the major benefits afforded by 401(k) plans. As we have already discussed, since you don't have to pay tax on your account's earnings until you withdraw funds, every penny you contribute and every penny earned works for your retirement. If you don't work for a company that offers a retirement plan (including a 401(k) plan), your entire $2,000 contribution is deductible, providing you yet another tax advantage. Eventually, when you begin withdrawing funds from your IRA, the money you take out is taxed as ordinary earnings—just as your 401(k) distributions will be taxed.

If, on the other hand, you (or your spouse) participate in an employer-sponsored retirement plan, you will face limits upon how much of your contribution you can deduct. As of the year 2000, single taxpayers who earn up to $32,000 and married taxpayers (filing joint income tax returns) who earn up to $52,000 can deduct the entire $2,000 contribution. Above those income limits, the deductibility is phased out to the point where contributions are no longer deductible for single taxpayers making more than $42,000 and married taxpayers making more than $62,000.

For the next several years, thanks to changes enacted in 1997, the income ranges for deductibility of contributions increase by nearly 60%, so that even if you cannot deduct your contributions now, you may be able to do so in the near future. The following chart shows the deductibility phase-out ranges through 2007.

Year	Single Taxpayer	Married, Filing Jointly
2001	$33,000-$43,000	$53,000-$63,000
2002	$34,000-$44,000	$54,000-$64,000
2003	$40,000-$50,000	$60,000-$70,000
2004	$45,000-$55,000	$65,000-$75,000
2005	$50,000-$60,000	$70,000-$80,000
2006	$50,000-$60,000	$75,000-$85,000
2007	$50,000-$60,000	$80,000-$100,000

During much of its lifetime, the traditional IRA did not allow contributions by a non-working spouse. The rules say you can contribute $2,000 or 100% of your income, *whichever is lower*. With the enactment of new rules in the Taxpayer Relief Act of 1997, though, a non-working spouse can contribute $2,000 and deduct the entire amount, even if the other partner participates in a company retirement plan. Naturally, though, the government limits even that deductibility for couples who have higher incomes. For joint incomes above $150,000, the contribution is only partially deductible, and when the joint income reaches $160,000, the deduction disappears entirely. However, regardless of your income, you can still contribute to the IRA without getting the deduction.

Like your 401(k) plan, traditional IRAs limit withdrawals before age 59½, unless you are willing to incur tax penalties of 10% of any monies received. Similarly, at the other end of the age scale, you have to begin withdrawing funds by April 1 (who chose that date?) of the year after the year you turn 70½ or you'll face other penalties. There are a couple of exceptions to the tax penalty for withdrawals, but before I mention them, remember one thing—this is your *retirement* account! Even before age 59½ you can withdraw penalty-free up to $10,000 for a first-time home purchase. On top of that, funds you withdraw for higher education—that's college and above—will also be spared the 10% early withdrawal penalty. However, under no circumstances do you avoid the regular income tax that will be applied to every cent you withdraw.

Traditional IRAs are simple to open. You can do it at your bank, through another financial institution, with a mutual fund or life insurance company, through your stock broker, or through your retirement advisor. You can open your IRA at any time, but the account must be established by the end of the calendar year for contributions to be deductible on that year's income tax return. There is, however, an added deductibility bonus. Once you establish your account, you can—within the allowable limits—deduct any contributions you make before your income tax return is due (not including extensions). So if you want to deduct contributions on your 2000 income tax return, you can make them as late as April 15, 2001. In fact, you can deduct the contributions even before you actually make them (for example, you file early and make your contribution on April 15th). Just be certain to tell your IRA sponsor for which year you are making the contribution.

When you shop for the right place to open your IRA, look for the same features and services we discussed in Chapter 5. In addition, consider the fees you'll be charged by your IRA holder to keep your money for the next ten or twenty years. Keep in mind that the goal is to make money, not to spend it. You want lots of features and services, with a minimum of fees and hidden costs. Make every dollar work for your retirement.

Roth IRAs

The Roth IRA, named for Senator William Roth of Delaware, came out of the provisions of the Taxpayer Relief Act of 1997. Available only since the beginning of 1998, Roth IRAs allow contributions of up to $2,000 per year (if you have earned at least that much), so long as your adjusted gross income does not exceed $95,000 for single taxpayers or $150,000 for married taxpayers filing jointly. The amount you can contribute phases out between $95,000 and $110,000 income for single taxpayers and between $150,000 and $160,000 income for married taxpayers filing jointly. Above those ranges, you're not allowed to have a Roth IRA. In addition, the amount you would be able to contribute to a Roth IRA is reduced dollar-for-dollar by any amount you contribute to a traditional IRA. Finally, it's important to note that contributions to a Roth IRA, unlike contributions to your 401(k) plan or your traditional IRA, are never tax-deductible.

The Roth IRA offers considerable advantages over the traditional IRA. Perhaps most significant is the potential of making withdrawals from your Roth IRA completely tax free. That's right, tax free. After leaving your money in your IRA for only five years after you establish your Roth IRA or five years after you roll over non-Roth IRA funds into the account, you can begin to withdraw the account's earnings completely tax free so long as you reach age 59½, become disabled, or—for your heirs—you die.

In fact, you can make early withdrawals any time without facing that nasty 10% tax penalty provided you withdraw only what you have contributed and not the earnings. So you could conceivably withdraw up to $2,000 per year of contributions to buy a car, take a vacation, or whatever. Of course, you shouldn't do that—it's for retirement, remember?

Three other features distinguish Roth IRAs from traditional IRAs. One, nothing requires you to begin withdrawing from your Roth IRA at any particular age—if ever. With traditional IRAs, you must begin to withdraw a required minimum distribution (RMD) from your account no later than April first of the year following the year in which you turn 70½. With the Roth IRA, you never have to withdraw the money.

Two, as long as you continue to earn an income, you can make contributions to your Roth IRA. Not so with the traditional IRA. When you reach that magical 70½ years, you must stop contributing (and, as we said, start withdrawing).

And three, money withdrawn from your Roth IRA does not count as taxable income, so it cannot make your Social Security benefits taxable by pushing you over the taxability threshold. Withdrawals from traditional IRAs, on the other hand, are included in taxable income and can put you over those limits.

One final benefit of the Roth IRA. At any age, once the account has been established for at least 5 years, you can withdraw a lifetime maximum of $10,000 for a first-time home purchase without incurring any taxes or penalties.

Under certain circumstances, you can even convert your existing IRA to a Roth IRA. The basic rule is that rollovers are allowed once per year when your adjusted gross income does not exceed $100,000 (regardless of whether you are single or are married, filing jointly). That's the good news. The bad news is, the taxable amount rolled over from your traditional IRA will be included in your income during the year of the transfer.

In short, a Roth IRA beats the traditional IRA by several comparisons. If you meet the income limits of a Roth IRA, you should probably choose it over an investment in a traditional IRA. The same organizations that will sell you a traditional IRA, will also sell you a Roth IRA, and the same considerations of features and services apply in your selection decision.

The following table provides a side-by-side comparison of the important features of Roth and traditional IRAs.

	Roth IRA	**Traditional IRA**
Eligibility	Anyone with earned income below these limits— Single: AGI* of $110,000. Married filing jointly: AGI of $160,000	Anyone with earned income under the age of 70½ (as of December 31 of the tax year)
Annual Contributions	Maximum $2,000 if single with AGI of $95,000 or less. Maximum $4,000 if married filing jointly with AGI of $150,000 or less.	Maximum $2,000 or 100% of earned income, whichever is less. Non-working spouse may also contribute $2,000.
Withdrawals / Distributions	No mandatory withdrawal age. No withdrawals until age 59½ (with some exceptions) and account has been in existence 5 years. May take lump-sum or withdraw in installments.	Must begin withdrawals no later than April 1 of the year after the year you reach age 70½. No withdrawals until age 59½ (with some exceptions). May take lump-sum or withdraw in installments.
Tax Deductions	No deductions allowed.	Fully deductible if: Neither you nor your spouse participated in a company-sponsored retirement plan OR if you contributed to such a plan, but you are: single with AGI $32,000 or less OR married filing jointly with AGI $52,000 or less (2000)

*AGI=Adjusted Gross Income

Taxes and Limitations	No earnings withdrawals until age 59½ (with some exceptions). No income tax on withdrawals after age 59½.	No withdrawals until age 59½ (with some exceptions). Must start withdrawing by age 70½ to avoid penalties. Withdrawals of all earnings and pretax dollars taxed as ordinary income.
Conversions	May convert from traditional IRA to Roth IRA if AGI is $100,000 or less. Direct rollovers from qualified retirement plans are not allowed.	Direct rollovers from qualified retirement plans are tax-free.

Rollover IRAs

Rollover IRAs are not a special type of IRA. They are simply IRAs into which you transfer other qualified retirement accounts. At some point—because of a change of employment or because of retirement, for example—you may be forced (or simply choose) to remove the investments from your existing 401(k) account. The best place to "roll over" those investments is an IRA, where the money can continue to appreciate tax-deferred.

Both traditional IRAs and Roth IRAs may be used for this purpose. The principal initial consideration in making this choice involves taxes. When a 401(k) account's balance is transferred directly into a rollover IRA of the traditional sort, there are no immediate tax consequences. You open an account with the IRA sponsor, and your 401(k) account assets get transferred directly to the new IRA account.

When you transfer your 401(k) assets to a Roth IRA, the procedure requires first a rollover to a traditional IRA, then conversion to a Roth IRA. When that conversion takes place, however, the tax consequences are considerable. Although there is no 10% penalty, the entire amount transferred to the Roth IRA gets taxed immediately as regular income. So, if you can't pay the tax, don't make the conversion.

We will revisit the issue of rollover IRAs in Chapter 7 when we discuss what to do with your 401(k) account when you leave your company or retire.

Using Your IRA and Your 401(k) Together

Assuming you can afford to save in both vehicles, there is no reason not to have both a 401(k) account and an IRA. Employing both types of accounts whenever you can increases the amount of money you can protect from erosion by current or future taxes. It should be easy to see that you can protect the growth on up to an additional $2,000 annually from current taxes by investing in a traditional IRA and untold amounts in future taxes by investing in a Roth IRA. By protecting your retirement investment against taxes, you increase the ultimate value of your retirement nest egg. Even beyond tax savings, though, recall from Chapter 1 the huge difference in the future value of your retirement account that an additional $2,000 investment each year could make. So after you have maximized your contribution to your 401(k), at least up to the full extent matched by your employer, if you can still afford to (and are qualified to) invest in an IRA of either sort, do so. It can't hurt.

If you invest in an IRA in addition to your 401(k), there are two considerations to keep in mind—one present and one future. The present consideration applies regardless of which IRA you choose: asset allocation. When you determine the best asset allocation strategy for your unique retirement planning needs, remember to include your IRA in the efficient frontier allocation model. Depending upon the particular IRA you have chosen, either of the following options may be employed to enable your IRA to complement your 401(k) account. First, if your IRA consists of a single style of mutual fund, count it as that type of asset in your investment planning. For example, if the efficient frontier model for your retirement portfolio suggests allocating 20% of your investments to small stocks and you intend to invest a total of $10,000 a year in retirement accounts, you could contribute $2,000 to your IRA (or Roth IRA) that consists only of a small stock mutual fund. And since most 401(k)s don't offer the full spectrum of asset classes, this might be a good way to diversify.

Second, if your IRA trustee is a mutual fund company affording you the ability to spread your investment among a range of mutual funds, you should allocate your IRA contributions in the same proportions as your 401(k) contributions. In other words, simply follow exactly the same asset allocation model that applies to your 401(k) account.

Either allocation model works. What's important is to remember that you have an IRA and that it's make-up should be consistent with the asset allocation determined by your own efficient frontier model. Otherwise, you may be adding more risk than return to your retirement portfolio.

The future consideration regards taxes. When the time comes to live on your retirement accounts, distributions taken from your 401(k) account and from a traditional IRA will be fully taxable as income when they are received. Therefore, you will have to withdraw somewhat more than one dollar for every dollar in living expense you expect to encounter. Distributions from your Roth IRA, however, are received tax-free—every dollar received can be used to cover expenses. Depending upon your income level, this difference can amount to 15% or 33% or—thanks to the government's ability to change the tax rate on a whim— even more. Be certain to consider both current and future taxes when making your selection of the IRA best suited to your expected circumstances.

Individual Retirement Accounts can work hand in hand with your 401(k) plan to maximize the value of your retirement assets. Used wisely, these accounts can save you taxes now and in the future and provide you a larger stream of income years from now. While your main priority should be to contribute to your 401(k) plan to the limits of your ability and the rules, investing in an IRA should also be among your prime objectives.

Years from now, after having invested thousands of dollars in retirement accounts of various sorts, you will want to begin to harvest the fruits of all your hard work. How you organize your harvest is every bit as important as how you sowed your investment seeds in the first place. In Chapter 7, we'll cover harvesting strategies. What are your options when you change companies? What's the best strategy when you finally do retire? How can you maximize the lifetime of your retirement portfolio? All these questions—and more—will be answered in the next chapter. So what are you waiting for?

The Scarborough Plan

1. Define in detail your retirement lifestyle.
2. Calculate exactly how much you'll need in your retirement account.
3. Determine how long it will be before you must tap into your retirement assets.
4. Start saving the required amounts now.
5. Determine your estimated Social Security income.
6. After your 401(k), rank your other investments according to the tax advantages they offer.
7. Invest your retirement savings in tax-deferred alternatives first.
8. Start investing now. The sooner you begin, the more you earn.

9. Invest regularly to gain the benefits of dollar cost averaging.
10. Diversify your assets appropriately to maximize your returns for a given level of risk.
11. Maximize the contributions—yours and your employer's—to your 401(k) plan.
12. Minimize the withdrawals from your 401(k) account.
13. Understand the options offered by your 401(k) plan.
14. Seek improvements in your 401(k) plan where necessary.
15. **Supplement your retirement accounts with an IRA for increased tax deferral.**
16. **If you qualify, invest in a Roth IRA.**
17. **Be sure to include your IRA monies in your overall asset allocation plan.**

SECTION III
WHAT TO DO
WITH ALL YOU'VE SAVED

7

WHAT YOU DO WHEN YOU RETIRE

I see two sorts of people every week who need help figuring out what to do with their 401(k) now that they're leaving their companies. There are people like Ed. He's 38, and he's moving to the fourth company of his career. "Mike," Ed said, "I've got three 401(k)s now. What should I do with them?"

And there are people like Barry. He's 57, retired, and doesn't really need his money yet. "How do I manage this stuff, Mike?" he asks.

At some point, you will begin to reap the rewards of all your retirement planning. How you manage your after-retirement use of your portfolio requires every bit as much planning as it did to create it. Beginning to make withdrawals without assessing your entire situation is one sure way of depleting your accounts faster than necessary. Invest plenty of time in evaluating your situation after retirement. Understand your options, whether you are retiring from all income-producing work or simply "retiring" to another company. Your goal during retirement is the same as your goal in preparing for retirement: maximize the power of your 401(k) plan to ensure that you and your family will enjoy the lifestyle you want.

Evaluating Your Situation After Retirement

Determining how best to manage your retirement resources comes down to understanding your ABCs: assets, beneficiaries, and circumstances. The range of asset types will dictate how complicated your planning post-retirement will be. You will probably have savings, an investment portfolio, real estate, and possibly other assets, plus your 401(k) account, your IRA, Social Security benefits, and other retirement accounts. Your beneficiaries must also be considered to the extent that they depend upon you for their living expenses (or that you depend upon their retirement savings or other assets for your combined living expenses). Finally, circumstances play a significant role in your retirement planning after your retire—your health, the success you achieved in building your retirement portfolio, the economy, and so on.

Assets. By the time you retire, you should already have made a formal record of all your assets: what they are, what they are worth, and where they are. With any luck, you'll have some combination of the following asset types:

◆ Pension (defined benefit) plan

◆ 401(k) plan

◆ Stocks, stock options, and ESOPs (employee stock ownership plans)

◆ Cash

◆ Individual Retirement Account(s) (IRAs)

◆ Your personal securities portfolio

◆ Insurance

◆ Annuities

◆ Real estate

◆ Inheritances and trusts

While you may not have everything on this list—or you

may have things that don't appear on this list—it's critical that you know what you have. Knowing what you have enables you to plan the order in which you begin to liqui-date your assets.

All along, one of the principal goals of your retirement planning has been to delay as long as possible the pay-ment of taxes, not out of any lack of patriotism, but simply because you want every penny of your assets working for you. Throughout your retirement years, the same principle applies: pay taxes only when you absolutely must. Using your assets wisely will guarantee that you pay taxes later, presumably at a time when you will be in the lower income tax brackets and pay less than you might today.

Before drawing on any other source of retirement funds, use cash. Not only has it already been taxed, but also it probably earns a lower rate of return than any of your other investments.

It makes sense, then, to rely first on those resources that have already been taxed or that will receive favorable tax treatment (e.g., long-term capital gains tax) when you use them. In other words, before anything else, use cash. Not only has it already been taxed, but also it probably earns a lower rate of return than any of your other invest-ments (with the possible exception of your real estate, which you may need). Although it is not generally wise to exhaust all your cash savings (you should always have emergency cash in reserve), the fact that it costs you no taxes and earns you little return makes cash the obvious first choice to pay the utilities and buy the groceries.

To make your liquidation planning easier, then, you should organize your list of assets into categories, as follows:

1. Assets that have already been taxed and won't be taxed again: cash, checking accounts, savings accounts, and the like.

2. Assets that will receive favorable tax treatment when you sell them: stocks and bonds held for more than one year, your primary residence, and so on.

3. Assets that will be taxed as ordinary income when you liquidate them: 401(k) accounts, IRAs, and others.

Generally speaking, you should liquidate your assets as necessary to maintain your lifestyle in the order listed above.

Beneficiaries. While you were employed, you most likely listed your spouse as your primary beneficiary for all your retirement accounts. (Unless exempted by your spouse, he or she must be your 401(k)—but not your IRA— beneficiary.) Now that you're retired, you need to reexamine those decisions about beneficiaries. Designating beneficiaries in accordance with the reality of who depends upon you for support should be a top priority. Well before you arrive at a time when your assets will be distributed among your heirs, you should consider how best to divide them. Will you be survived by your spouse? By your children? By your parents? By grandchildren? Far better for you to determine who receives what than for your executor to guess what your wishes might have been.

Life being what it is, though, other events could transpire that affect your designation of beneficiaries. Even in retirement, divorce and death happen. What becomes of your retirement assets should you and your spouse divorce? Are your joint assets likely to be divided equally? Do you both have retirement assets—pensions, Social Security, 401(k) accounts, and IRAs—of your own? Would you be able to maintain your chosen lifestyle on the share of your retirement assets you'd likely receive if you divorced? A surprising number of people find themselves facing these questions after retirement, and few of them are prepared for the answers they arrive at.

What happens should your spouse die? Will you receive the balance of his/her defined benefit plans? How much are the Social Security benefits that will accrue to you? Are you the designated beneficiary of his/her various assets (not only insurance, but also pensions, retirement accounts, and so on)? Do you have adequate insurance to take care of the funeral bills? Except in rare circumstances, either you or your spouse will die first (not together), so you both have to be prepared for whoever remains after the other one dies. Consult your lawyer, financial advisor, spouse—whomever it takes—to get answers to these important questions.

How do you and your spouse coordinate your 401(k) accounts and IRAs? Because there is no effective way of combining your accounts, someone (one or both of you or somebody else working for the two of you) needs to keep track of the accounts to be sure that your overall asset allocation makes sense and is maintained. You will both benefit from having a concerted approach to asset allocation rather than a haphazard process. It would not serve either of you if your spouse's retirement assets were ideally allocated and your half of the retirement pot was fully invested in highly-volatile Internet stocks. Sit down together, preferably along with your financial advisor, and map out a joint asset allocation program to ensure you maximize the power of your combined retirement assets.

Finally, consider how you might minimize the impact of taxes when you die. Decisions you make before you die can reduce the taxes your heirs pay on your hard-earned assets. Your situation may be such that establishing trusts for your various beneficiaries makes sense. Or it may make sense for you to make regular, tax-free gifts to your spouse or children as part of their inheritance before you die. Any of these decisions require careful consideration and, often, professional advice from financial planners, accountants, and attorneys. Although it may not matter to you at that time, you can still minimize the amount of taxes your estate must pay. And that means more for your heirs.

Circumstances. Along with assets and beneficiaries, specific circumstances after you retire will dictate how you manage your retirement accounts. Prime among your considerations will be whether or not you were successful in meeting your retirement financial goals. If you have set aside amounts equaling or exceeding those planned for, then you should be able to follow your original plan for withdrawing funds when the time comes. If you planned on needing $40,000 a year, for example, and you succeeded in amassing the necessary principal to earn that (plus inflation) each year, give yourself a pat on the back.

Success in achieving your financial goals for retirement must also be balanced with success in keeping your expenses to the anticipated level, too. For that reason, unanticipated expenses could throw off all your well-laid plans. If you did not adequately plan for the possibility of serious illness in yourself or in those dependent upon you, for example, health care costs could severely deplete the funds you need to live the rest of your life in style. Inflation in excess of what you expected could also have increased your expenses to a level unforeseen in your retirement planning. And, of course, economic conditions could have been wildly different from what you assumed in your planning process. In short, when the time comes, you must also reassess your financial needs to determine whether your resources are sufficient to support the planned for lifestyle.

Having completed your post-retirement ABCs, it's time to examine what your alternatives are in taking distributions from your 401(k) plan. We'll explore your choices under two circumstances: (1) when you change jobs and (2) when you retire (for good) from your job. Your main objectives under either scenario include minimizing the tax impacts of any withdrawal and maximizing your control of the assets in your 401(k) account. Always bearing these objectives in mind will simplify your decision-making processes.

What If You "Retire" to Another Job?

When you change jobs, you have four main alternatives for what to do with your 401(k) account:

♦ Take a lump sum distribution.

♦ Leave the 401(k) account where it is.

♦ Transfer the 401(k) account to your new company's 401(k) plan.

♦ Transfer the 401(k) assets to a rollover IRA.

Let's explore each of these alternatives in turn.

You could take a lump sum distribution. For several reasons, this is probably the least attractive of the four alternatives. First, you'll face an immediate 20% withholding to cover potential taxes. The government simply won't take your promise that you're going to put the funds into a rollover IRA within sixty days (the limit to avoid full taxation and penalty). Second, you have to rely on your discipline to actually roll over the funds into an IRA. If you don't, you will have to pay not only regular income taxes on the full amount, but also the infamous 10% tax penalty for early withdrawal. The only exceptions apply to you if you're already fifty-five years old or if you're taking the money out in payments designed to last a lifetime. These, in any case, would not be a lump sum distribution, anyway. They are called 72(t) distributions. Right off the bat, then, you could lose upwards of half your 401(k)'s value by taking a lump sum distribution. There are certainly reasons, though, when you might take the lump sum (seed money for a new business, say). But do this only as a last resort. Better yet, you probably shouldn't do it at all.

Your second option would be to leave the 401(k) right where it is, with the old employer. Unless your account is worth less than $5,000, the company must allow you to leave it there if you so choose. There are few advantages to leaving the account where it is (saving a few signatures on transfer forms is about all) and some possible disadvantages. On the positive side, the old company's services could be better, the asset options might not be available elsewhere, and the management fees might be cheaper. On the negative side, the old company's plan might be inferior to the new company's plan. Still, leaving the funds where they are until you find a better place to move them is perfectly acceptable. They're less likely to disappear than they would be if you kept them in your pocket, that's certain!

You could move your 401(k) account to your new employer's 401(k) plan. The way you exercise this option is to enroll in your new employer's 401(k) plan first, then execute an institution-to-institution transfer form allowing the old company to move your 401(k) assets to your new company. In virtually every situation, your old assets will be liquidated and transferred to your new account as cash, where they will be distributed according to your new asset allocation designations. It is extremely unlikely that your new company will offer exactly the same investment choices as your old company; hence, the necessity of transferring your assets as cash. Don't worry, though. The IRS considers this to be a tax-free transfer of funds, so you will face neither immediate taxes nor penalties in association with the move.

Two possible disadvantages accompany a company-to-company transfer. First, as mentioned, your investment selection may differ substantially, in which case your old asset allocation scheme might not apply and you will have to establish a new allocation in light of the new choices. The range of choices may be more limited. Second, your

new company might have a service requirement to participate in its 401(k) plan—you could face up to a 12-month
wait before you can effect the transfer of your account.
Often, however, these eligibility requirements are waived
for company-to-company transfers. Generally, these potential disadvantages should not preclude this option. You
should already have known about the new 401(k) plan and
its requirements before making the move and planned accordingly. And, if you do face a service requirement, you
can always leave the 401(k) account with the old company
until you meet the participation requirement.

On the other hand, transferring your 401(k) account
to your new employer offers one big advantage in the form
of simplicity and consolidation. It will be easier to maintain your asset allocation plan if you have only one account to keep track of, rather than two (or more) 401(k)
accounts, plus an IRA here and there. For many people,
this advantage gives it an edge over the fourth alternative.

Finally, you could have your 401(k) account value
transferred directly into a rollover IRA. By having your old
company transfer the funds directly to the rollover IRA,
you avoid the withdrawal, taxes, and penalties associated
with having the company write the check to you. As with
an institution-to-institution transfer, you must first establish the rollover IRA with a bank, broker, or investment
institution (like a mutual fund company). After establishing the account, execute the necessary forms to transfer
your 401(k) assets into the new IRA.

This option offers a number of advantages over the
others. Principal among them are the flexibility and control you gain from being able to manage your retirement
account directly. Rather than settle for the limited investment selections offered by many 401(k) plans, you can select from a broad range of investment categories by establishing an IRA. Most mutual fund companies and brokers
provide a vast array of asset selections. And virtually every
mutual fund company allows redistributions of assets into

other investment alternatives at little or no cost, within certain restrictions.

It's worth reiterating the importance of the mechanism you should use for transferring funds into your rollover IRA. Have the old company write (and mail) a check directly to the institution that holds your new account. Otherwise, if you were to have the old company write the check to you, the old company would withhold 20% of the value for potential taxes. Nevertheless, you would still—within sixty days—have to deposit the full 100% of value into your new rollover IRA. In other words, you'd have to come up with that extra 20%, because you won't see it again until you file your income taxes and—you hope—get your tax refund. And if, for some reason, you neglect to redeposit the money within the required sixty days, you'll be stuck with regular income taxes plus a hefty penalty of 10% of the closing account value. This decision is a no brainer— have the old company write a check to your new rollover IRA. It's simpler, and it's safer.

Among these four choices, taking a lump sum distribution is clearly the worst, because of the tax consequences and because of the temptation to spend, rather than to invest, it. Leaving the account where it is—with your old employer—might be reasonable, particularly if the range of investments is broad, the performance of the funds has been good, or the management costs or plan features are better. Transferring your 401(k) account to your new company's 401(k) plan represents a reasonable second choice, assuming the plan itself satisfies the criteria presented in Chapter 5 for good 401(k) plans. In most cases, your best bet will be to transfer your 401(k) assets into a rollover IRA, where you can readily keep track of the funds and make the asset allocation adjustments whenever necessary.

What If You Retire From All Work?

Not surprisingly, your alternatives upon retirement are

similar to those you face when changing employers. The only one of the four previously described options not available is the transfer of your 401(k) account to another 401(k) plan, because you are not changing employers. You still have the other three choices—taking a lump sum distribution, leaving the account where it is, and transferring the account to a rollover IRA. But now, the implications are somewhat different since you're leaving employment forever (you hope).

There may be circumstances where taking a lump sum distribution is not completely unwise. For example, if you meet the income guidelines for a conversion Roth IRA, it's conceivable that taking a lump sum distribution, paying the ordinary income taxes, and then depositing what's left in a Roth IRA might make sense. Sure, you take a big tax hit right at the outset, but every subsequent withdrawal will be free of taxation. And unlike regular IRAs, a Roth IRA carries no age limit at which you must begin to take withdrawals. If, after consulting your retirement planner, the Roth IRA looks like the way to go, you'll have to transfer your 401(k) account assets into a rollover IRA first—direct rollovers from qualified retirement plans into Roth IRAs are not allowed.

What about leaving your 401(k) account where it is, with the company from which you just retired? Leaving the account with the former employer has certain benefits. There may be unique investment options offered by your employer that cannot be found anywhere else. This is unlikely, but possible. Another advantage is simplicity—as mentioned earlier, leaving the account where it is saves you having to make decisions about which IRA is best for you and then transferring the funds to the new account. Finally, you might consider one legal advantage of leaving your 401(k) account where it is. If, for some reason, you anticipate the possibility of going bankrupt, your funds are better off in your old employer's 401(k) plan—they're protected from your creditors there, but not necessarily in an

IRA. With an IRA, you also lose the ability to borrow from the account.

If you leave your account where it is, you will have to make decisions about how to begin taking distributions. Remember that the rules require that you begin taking money from your account by April 1 of the year following the calendar year in which you turn 70½ unless you are still working. How you can take those distributions will be discussed below.

Transferring your funds to a rollover IRA usually represents the wisest choice when you retire. By exercising this option, you may increase the availability to you of the funds in your retirement account while continuing to preserve its tax deferral status until you withdraw funds. This alternative enables you to withdraw funds as necessary and to reallocate the assets as you and your retirement advisor see fit. Plus, all the aforementioned advantages apply—range of investment types, flexibility, and so on.

In fact, transferring all your 401(k) accounts—remember, you're likely to have several—into a single rollover IRA enables you to consolidate all your retirement assets into one account, where management is easier and more efficient. You will only have one account report to make sense of, and you'll find it far easier to maintain your asset allocation strategy. Moving all your retirement assets into one good, well-allocated rollover IRA makes great sense. Alternatively, you might employ several IRAs for two reasons. First, you could use multiple IRAs with different beneficiaries to be sure your money goes exactly where you want it when you're gone. Second you could employ several IRAs for the purpose of laddering (or staggering) those 72(t) distributions I mentioned earlier.

What do you do with your rollover IRA account after you retire? You manage it every bit as carefully as you did before you retired. That means keeping track of its performance, establishing and maintaining a sensible allocation of assets (which will change with retirement, as we discussed in Chapter 3), and keeping expenses to a minimum.

But it also means managing your withdrawals in such a way that your account is there for you whenever you need it, from now on.

Maximizing the Lifetime of Your Retirement Portfolio

In the very first chapter, I suggested that you plan as if you were going to live forever. Once you reach retirement, you need to maintain that posture of expectancy. Don't assume you'll live to 75 or 80 or 100. Assume you'll live forever and manage your assets accordingly. In other words, plan to die with more assets than you retire with. You can do that by maintaining the sound strategy of financial management you pursued in the years before retirement.

Yes, I realize this strategy is not for everyone. But even if (or especially if) your planning is based on the oldest-relative-plus-ten expectation, I cannot overemphasize the importance of sticking with the methods that carried you this far.

First, continue to see that your portfolio produces at maximum efficiency. Allocate your assets—in accordance with a more conservative risk-return profile—so that your portfolio lives right smack on the efficient frontier. Retirement is no excuse to settle for less than the best returns you can get for a given level of risk, even though the acceptable risk might be a bit lower now. Judiciously watch those asset allocations and keep them matched to your plan.

Plan your withdrawals with the goal of never touching your principal value—or, if necessity dictates, of maintaining the value as long as possible.

Next, carefully plan your withdrawals with the goal of never touching your principal value—or, if necessity dictates, of maintaining the value as long as possible. We already discussed this concept, but it's worth reiterating. Plan your withdrawals in such a way that your assets continue to grow, or at the very least, so that your account value remains constant (in current dollars) from year to year. Here's how we said to do that in Chapter 1. First, determine how much your account will be able to earn each year, on average. Subtract from that amount the long-term rate of inflation, about 3%. What's left is the percentage of your portfolio you can afford to withdraw each year and still maintain a level principal value adjusted upward for inflation. As we said in Chapter 1, if you can earn about 8.5% year in and year out, you can afford to withdraw about 5.5% of your portfolio value each year without the principal eroding in value. Each $100,000 in account value, then, should provide you around $5,500 in expendable income annually. Since the account value will increase, the amount you can withdraw each year should increase with inflation. Realize that returns vary from year to year, so there will be times where you will eat into principal due to bad years. Don't significantly change the draw in good years or bad. Instead, reassess the situation periodically and try to stick with a steady level of withdrawal.

Once you reach age 70½, the situation changes (unless you are still working), and you must begin to take withdrawals from your tax-deferred retirement accounts. For 401(k) accounts, companies generally offer four options for withdrawing the money: (1) lump sum distribution, (2) annuitizing your 401(k), (3) term-certain contracts, or (4) installments. Lump sum distribution we've already discussed at some length. Unless your account balance is pitifully small, you'd only take this withdrawal choice if you were immediately rolling the funds into a rollover IRA. Otherwise, the tax implications make it unwise.

Alternatively, you can choose to have your company

annuitize your 401(k) distributions. You can choose either a single-life annuity (where the payments continue for the rest of your life) or joint-and-survivor annuity (where the payments continue as long you or your spouse lives). Joint-and-survivor annuities are generally smaller by 10% to 15%, a small price to pay for a guaranteed income throughout both your remaining lives. In either case, the amount of the payment is determined by a calculation based on the balance in your 401(k) account, the prevailing interest rates, and your life expectancy. With this distribution method, the full remaining amount of your 401(k) account is distributed to your estate, which must pay income taxes on the amount distributed.

Term-certain contracts, instead of relying upon when you or your spouse actually die, guarantee the payouts for a specified number of years. In other words, you can elect to designate that payments continue over a 5-, 10-, or 20-year period regardless of whether you are alive to receive them. This offers the advantage of delaying the time at which your estate is forced to pay income taxes. This option is available only if you elect it in writing before April 1 of the year following the year in which you turn 70½, but for most individuals the term-certain distribution is better than annuitizing.

Finally, you can also arrange to receive your 401(k) distributions as a series of set installments. In this method, you receive the payments until the account is fully depleted. Some plans allow modifications in the installment payouts and some don't, so be sure you know what you're getting into if you choose this distribution method. Depending upon the plan, you may not be allowed to change your mind once the installments begin. And your ability to make asset allocation decisions may be limited. For these reasons, installment payouts represent an inferior alternative to rolling your account into an IRA.

For rollover (and other) IRA distributions, the alternatives are essentially the same. The exception, as previously described, is the distribution of Roth IRA assets. The lack of a requirement to begin taking funds at any particular age—if ever—means you can leave assets in the Roth IRA indefinitely. In many cases, the Roth IRA will prove to be a superior vehicle for leaving assets to your heirs in a form that avoids income taxes.

By this point, you may be thinking that some outside assistance would be a great help in assuring that you establish all the right goals and formulate a plan that makes sense. You may be thinking, *I could use professional help.* Professional retirement planning help, that is. You may be right. But how do you locate good help that you can afford. Where do you turn? To the next chapter, that's where. In Chapter 8, we'll discuss what to look for in retirement financial advisors and what you can expect to pay for their advice and services. Then you'll be fully prepared to identify the professional who can help you maximize the power of your 401(k) plan and achieve your retirement goals.

The Scarborough Plan

1. Define in detail your retirement lifestyle.
2. Calculate exactly how much you'll need in your retirement account.
3. Determine how long it will be before you must tap into your retirement assets.
4. Start saving the required amounts now.
5. Determine your estimated Social Security income.
6. After your 401(k), rank your other investments according to the tax advantages they offer.
7. Invest your retirement savings in tax-deferred alternatives first.
8. Start investing now. The sooner you begin, the more you earn.

9. Invest regularly to gain the benefits of dollar cost averaging.
10. Diversify your assets appropriately to maximize your returns for a given level of risk.
11. Maximize the contributions—yours and your employer's—to your 401(k) plan.
12. Minimize the withdrawals from your 401(k) account.
13. Understand the options offered by your 401(k) plan.
14. Seek improvements in your 401(k) plan where necessary.
15. Supplement your retirement accounts with an IRA for increased tax deferral.
16. If you qualify, invest in a Roth IRA.
17. Be sure to include your IRA monies in your overall asset allocation plan.
18. **After you retire, use those assets first that have already been taxed.**
19. **Formulate a distribution strategy that best matches your needs.**
20. **Employ sound financial management to maximize your principal's life.**

8

GETTING HELP WITH YOUR 401(k)

"I don't have time to do this, Mike. You take care of it for me." That's Jackie speaking – the CEO of a medium-sized company. Jackie, who knows all about financial management and is highly paid to run the affairs of a large and profitable company.

I get the same thing from plenty of bright people who, for whatever reason, say they don't have the time, knowledge, or inclination to manage their 401(k) accounts on their own. As helpful as this book may be, there are those of you who still want the comfort of having a professional financial advisor to help you manage the intricacies of your retirement planning. Professional advice is great, so long as you know what you're looking for, how to find it, and what you're going to have to pay for it. This chapter will help you figure out what you need from a 401(k) advisor; show you what to look for in a good advisor; provide some pointers on working with your financial advisor; and give you an idea of what such advice may cost you. After this chapter, you should be fully prepared to select an advisor who best fits your needs—and your budget.

And one more thing. Never feel embarrassed about seeking professional financial advice. None of us can know everything there is to know about retirement planning. It never hurts to ask an expert. Anything is better than simply making an initial decision about your 401(k) plan and then never looking at it again—and that's what surveys say most people do!

Why You Might Want a Financial Advisor

Besides the general comfort of knowing a professional is guiding you, there is a range of reasons you might seek financial advice. At one end of the spectrum, you might want a financial advisor to do everything from evaluating your current 401(k) situation to assembling your retirement strategy to executing the final retirement plan. At the other end, you might simply want someone who can field occasional questions about your on-going retirement strategy. Between these extremes are various individual aspects of your retirement planning that might need professional attention—like maximizing the power of your 401(k) plan, for example, by helping with asset allocation or creating your own personal efficient frontier. Others of you simply might not have the time to give your retirement planning the necessary attention to ensure its growth. And some of you may give it too much time—constantly making changes that ensure only that you miss the opportunity to achieve the greatest returns at the lowest risk level.

Beyond your 401(k) planning, other financial planning services you might consider are cash management and budgeting, tax planning, estate planning, insurance advice, and preparation of financial statements (net worth and so on). It helps to know what's available when you're assessing your own need for financial advice.

Before you start looking for a financial advisor, it will help to settle on what you need, because your needs will dictate the type of financial advisor you want. A comprehensive plan for your current and future financial situation may require the services of a financial planner, while intermittent consulting needs might be adequately met by your broker, banker, or accountant. If your needs are exclusively retirement-oriented, you should select someone whose business focuses on retirement planning. And if you want the best results with your 401(k) plan, seek the advice of experts who specialize in their optimization. Whatever your own requirements, be sure you match the right professional to your unique needs.

One way to be sure you know what you're looking for is to sit down and write in one sentence exactly what you want in the way of professional guidance. *I want somebody to tell me exactly how to allocate my assets, given my risk tolerance, in a way that will provide me the highest returns.* Or, *I want someone to evaluate my company's 401(k) plan and tell me if it's any good.* Or, *Now that I'm retired, I need help figuring out how much money I can take out every year without running out of funds.* Whatever your wants, you ought to be able to distill them into one sentence. Then, when you start interviewing advisor candidates, you need only convert your sentence into a question. Such as, *Can you tell me exactly how to allocate my assets, given my risk tolerance, in a way that will provide me the highest returns?* You get the idea.

Once you've figured out exactly what you need, the next step is determining who can provide it. Here are several types of financial advisors you're likely to encounter, along with a description of what they ought to be able to help you with:

- ◆ Certified Financial Planner (CFP). CFPs must complete an approved course of study, work at least three years in financial planning, and pass a rigorous exam on financial planning. CFPs can provide sound advice about managing all your finances—establishing goals and objectives, budgeting, investment planning, the whole works. The CFP is the person you want for comprehensive planning. Most have experience in retirement planning.

- Chartered Retirement Planning Counselor (CRPC). CRPCs can help you with all aspects of your retirement planning, from asset allocation to tax considerations.

- Chartered Financial Consultant (ChFC). ChFC certificates are earned by completing a specified course of study and passing an exam on personal finance from The American College in Bryn Mawr, Pennsylvania. These financial planners typically began their careers in the insurance industry, rather than in the investment industry.

- Certified Public Accountant (CPA). CPAs have been educated in accounting and have passed a stringent examination on accounting and tax preparation. This doesn't mean they know anything about investment and retirement counseling. The American Institute of CPAs does, however, certify those who meet certain requirements in the field of personal financial planning by designating them Personal Finance Specialists (PFS). A CPA-PFS, therefore, might offer the ideal combination of financial and tax planning.

- Registered Financial Consultant (RFC). Practicing financial consultants who meet strict requirements of education, experience, and integrity in financial services earn the RFC designation. Like their CFP and ChFC colleagues, they need to have additional expertise in retirement planning if you're going to entrust your retirement accounts to them.

As you can see, there are plenty of choices, but each designation has its own range of qualifications. Seek your advice from someone who's supposed to be qualified to dispense sound counsel.

What You Should Look for in a 401(k) Plan Advisor

Whereas any of the finance professionals might help you along with your 401(k) plan, your best bet is to identify someone well versed in all the topics I've covered in this book. Sure, experience with 401(k) plans will help, but a better range of knowledge and experience will bring you better results. Your top priority should be to identify someone who has helped others in your situation to evaluate their 401(k) plans, to determine how best to use their 401(k) plans to prepare for their retirement, and to figure out how to make their 401(k) plans and other assets work together for maximum benefit. How do you find such an advisor?

Since this person will be as important to your retirement portfolio's health as your physician is to your physical health, search with care. Ask the same people for referrals that you'd ask about a good doctor. Reasonable referral sources include family and friends, accountants, attorneys, bankers, insurance agents—maybe even your doctor. If that doesn't generate enough leads, call the local office of a financial planning association—the Financial Planning Association (a merger of the former International Association of Financial Planners and the Institute of Certified Financial Planners) is a good first step—and ask for a list of the financial planners in your area. You'll want to have several candidates for the job, so start with at least five names.

Before you start calling the people on your list and scheduling interviews, give some thought to the "softer" aspects of what you're seeking. Sure, you want somebody who's an expert at what you need. But you also want someone sufficiently compatible to endure a long partnership with you in managing your money. He or she should share—or at least understand—your ideas about how your money should be handled and about how communication between you should be maintained. And the advisor must understand that you're the boss, and he or she is working for you.

You'll probably want to screen your candidates by telephone. In fact, to get the best possible 401(k) advisor, telephone information may be all you need. Many communities have no such advisors, so you may find yourself relying on a 401(k) specialist in another community – or even out of state. Once they demonstrate to your satisfaction that they possess appropriate credentials, determine whether their experience and expertise match your needs. Ask every one of them the same set of questions. Here is a list you could start with. It's by no means exhaustive, so you'll want to add questions that pertain to your own situation.

♦ Have you ever been cited by any professional board or society for disciplinary reasons? Quite simply, you don't want your advisor doing anything illegal or unethical. If the advisor is also a Registered Representative (a broker), you can check for violations by phoning the National Association of Securities Dealers (NASD) at 1-800-289-9999 or by visiting their Public Disclosure Program web page at www.nasdr.com. If the advisor is a Registered Investment Advisor, you can check for problems at the Investor Assistant web page of the Securities and Exchange Commission at www.sec.gov.

♦ What specific financial planning services do you offer? Make sure the services offered satisfy your planning needs.

♦ Do you sell financial products (mutual funds, stocks, bonds, insurance, and the like)? If so, it's worth knowing what those products might cost you indirectly in terms of sales commissions paid back to the advisor.

♦ How long have you been in practice? Granted, longevity is no guarantee of expertise, but veterans are generally safer bets than novices.

♦ How do you charge for your services? Different advisors use different schemes for their services. Some charge a flat fee, others charge a commission based on the value of your portfolio. See below for more information regarding fees.

♦ How much attention will my account get? You want your advisor to take a proactive approach with your retirement accounts. What you don't want is for him or her to take a snapshot in time and never reassess your situation or adjust your allocations according to changing needs and conditions.

♦ Can you provide references? If the answer is no, you have to question whether it's worth including this advisor on your short list. If the answer is yes, take advantage of the chance to speak with current and/or past clients. You want to be able to check the validity of the answers the advisor gives you during this interview. You're less interested in the sorts of returns they have earned, though that kind of information should be sought. Instead, you want to know how well the advisor attends to the client's account and how effectively the advisor communicates with the client. Returns are important, but the quality of the relationship is paramount.

You may think of additional questions that apply to your situation and needs. Be sure to ask them—all of them—of each potential advisor you meet.

After you have interviewed all of the financial advisor candidates, assemble all your lists and answers and information. Give yourself plenty of time to review all the material, comparing both the objective information and your subjective impressions of the several candidates. You want to make the choice that best fits your needs. Keep in mind that the decision you make could have a big impact on the quality of your retirement years from now. Select an advisor you'll be comfortable with. You want to have no reservations about calling your 401(k) advisor with questions and concerns, so be sure it's someone you can trust and someone you can get along with.

How Best to Work With Your Advisor

Working with a financial advisor is a two-way endeavor. While you expect plenty of high quality advice from the advisor, he or she requires lots of accurate, detailed information from you in order to do a good job. When you schedule your first "real" consultation with the chosen advisor, ask what information he or she needs to be able to assess your situation effectively. Then provide that information. Don't hold back—if you do, you can count on your financial plan being incomplete, inaccurate, and ineffective. You presumably chose someone you trust as your advisor, so give him or her whatever he or she needs in order to provide you the best advice.

From your advisor you should expect several sorts of communication. First, you should receive a regular report regarding the status of your retirement accounts. If your advisor is guiding your 401(k) account decisions (or making them for you), ask for an explanation of your 401(k) account statement. Ask whether the specific fund choices still make sense (for example, *Is this the best mutual fund for my small company stock allocation?*) Ask whether your account value is growing in line with your goals and expectations.

Quarterly, or at least semiannually, your advisor should also review and discuss with you your asset allocations. It's unlikely that your allocation percentages will change significantly from quarter to quarter, but there's a good chance—as suggested by the example question above—that specific fund changes may be required to provide the best risk-return alternative within an investment class. Over time, asset allocations will change, as we discussed in Chapter 3.

In times of economic or political instability, your advisor should discuss with you what the best approach might be during the period of uncertainty. You might need to change your allocations temporarily; you might not. But your advisor should at least recognize the economic realities and tell you what response makes the most sense.

Throughout the relationship, communication should take place freely in both directions. Whenever you have a question, you should feel free to phone. And you should expect a timely response to your queries. Similarly, whenever your advisor calls, you should listen and provide whatever information or response is called for. Full communication ensures a good understanding and a sound relationship. Even if nothing seems to be changing, you and your advisor should touch base several times a year. And when situations are changing, frequent communication guarantees timely, appropriate decisions to maximize the value and safety of your retirement assets.

And speaking of communication, let me offer a few words on the proliferation of on-line (Internet) financial advisors, including those who purport to be experts on 401(k) plan management. One of the critical factors I mentioned earlier in selecting your 401(k) advisor was comfort. You need to feel free to call your advisor anytime to be able to get your questions answered. Internet-based services claim to provide such service 24 hours a day, 7 days a week. I have a couple of problems with this sort of approach to 401(k) planning.

First, what you'll find is that, more often than not, you're getting a computer program in place of a competent professional. Now if you're looking for interactive, fast-paced games, your computer might be just the place to go. But we're not playing games with your retirement assets. Your individual needs and concerns cannot be dealt with by a computer program that asks you a couple of questions. What you want is a personal 401(k) advisor who knows what questions to ask—and what questions to ask about the answers you give.

Second, the Internet abounds with so-called experts on everything. To tell you the truth, I don't know how you check out the credentials of a web site. Do you ever really know whom you're talking to? Even if you do, is it always the same "person" whenever you log on? When you phone your 401(k) advisor, you'd like to be able to hear the voice of the person you hired, the person you deemed competent to help you maximize the value of your 401(k) plan. You just can't get that on any web.

Sure, you can get information, plenty of it, on the Internet. You can find web sites that claim to be able to help you manage your 401(k) plan assets. But what you want is not virtual help, but the real thing. Find a competent 401(k) advisor you can be comfortable with—one with a face and a voice, neither of which is digitized.

What Your Advisor Will Charge You

Even before you begin to identify a 401(k) plan advisor, it helps to understand the basis for the fees you'll face. Three basic methods are common. When you need only intermittent advice, rather than actual management of your 401(k) plan, you might be expected to pay an hourly rate. You might favor this option if you expect to phone the advisor a few times a year with brief, specific questions that call for limited or no research and a quick answer. Anything more intensive than that should lead you to another billing option, because otherwise you can spend a lot of money over the course of a year, let alone over the years between now and your retirement. Why? Depending on the expertise of the advisor, you can expect to pay anywhere from $25 to $250 an hour. So it can add up faster than you'd think. What may seem like a five-minute phone call to you could generate an hour or more of service, billed at the appropriate rate.

Two other methods find more widespread acceptance among 401(k) plan advisors and their clients. One popular method involves charging you a flat fee for a given period of services. This method gives you the ability (and the comfort) to call your advisor whenever you have a question without worrying about how much it will cost you—you've already paid for the service. There are no surprises with this method—you know what you will receive in the way of services, and you know what you will have to pay.

For help with the strategies I've described in this book for maximizing the power of your 401(k) plan, you should expect to pay several hundred dollars per year. But if you have several 401(k) plans and a few IRAs and a defined benefit plan (pension plan) and various and sundry other retirement accounts, you can expect to pay a bit more until you can consolidate them into a few manageable accounts.

The third method bases the advisor's fee on the value of your portfolio. With this approach, your advisor shares in the benefits of sound advice. If you do well, your advisor does well. This approach is favored by financial planners, who often create a hybrid of the three methods. They may, for example, charge a small flat fee plus a percentage of assets under management. Alternatively, they may use different formulas for different products and services.

The key point to remember is this: know how your financial advisor charges for services, so you aren't surprised when the bill arrives.

Now that you have the tools to maximize the power of your 401(k), it's time to put them to work for you. Find an advisor who fits your personality, budget, and retirement planning needs and get started immediately.

The Scarborough Plan

1. Define in detail your retirement lifestyle.
2. Calculate exactly how much you'll need in your
   retirement account.

3. Determine how long it will be before you must tap into your retirement assets.

4. Start saving the required amounts now.

5. Determine your estimated Social Security income.

6. After your 401(k), rank your other investments according to the tax advantages they offer.

7. Invest your retirement savings in tax-deferred alternatives first.

8. Start investing now. The sooner you begin, the more you earn.

9. Invest regularly to gain the benefits of dollar cost averaging.

10. Diversify your assets appropriately to maximize your returns for a given level of risk.

11. Maximize the contributions—yours and your employer's—to your 401(k) plan.

12. Minimize the withdrawals from your 401(k) account.

13. Understand the options offered by your 401(k) plan.

14. Seek improvements in your 401(k) plan where necessary.

15. Supplement your retirement accounts with an IRA for increased tax deferral.

16. If you qualify, invest in a Roth IRA.

17. Be sure to include your IRA monies in your overall asset allocation plan.

18. After you retire, use those assets first that have already been taxed.

19. Formulate a distribution strategy that best matches your needs.

20. Employ sound financial management to maximize your principal's life.

21. Work with a trained professional 401(k) plan advisor who follows the principles in this book to maximize the power of your 401(k).